English Code 3

Activity Book

Contents

OUR WORLD

INTRO:
Here we stand: children of every age,
This is our world and the world's our stage.
We can laugh, we can cry — we can float, we can fly,
We can dance, we can sing — we can do almost anything
in OUR world ... our *beautiful* world.

VERSE 1:
Some of us are small; some of us are tall,
Some of us are shy; some say hi to everybody,
Some of us like numbers; some of us love words,
Some of us watch football, and some of us watch the birds!

(CHORUS)
This is our world ... we're different but the same.
We live and learn together — we get to know each other ...
in OUR world ... our *beautiful* world.

VERSE 2:
Some of us like music; some of us like cars,
Some of us draw pictures, looking at the stars,
Some of us are scientists, trying to find the code,
All of us can help a friend and give a hand to hold.

This is our world — there's room for everyone.
We learn to live together, and we have a lot of fun ...
In **our** world ... in **our** world ... in our beautiful world!

Progress Chart

You did it!

Congratulations!

Unit 8

Unit 7

Unit 6

Unit 5

Unit 4

Unit 3

Unit 2

Unit 1

Creativity

Collaboration

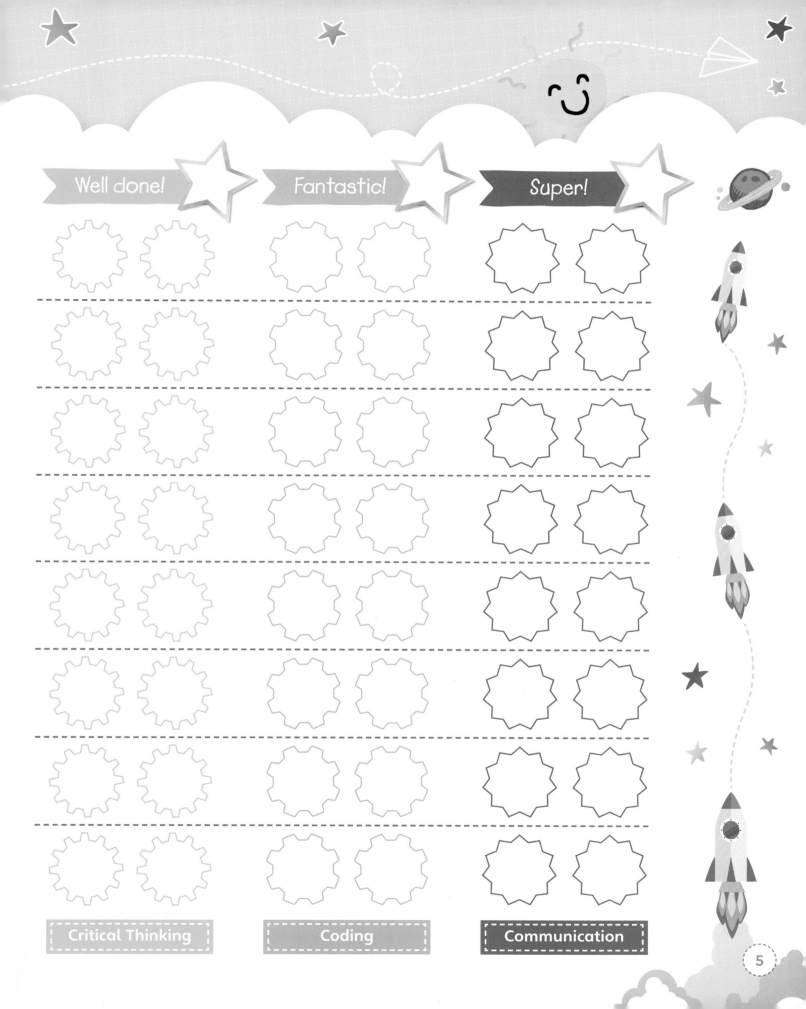

Well done!

Fantastic!

Super!

Critical Thinking

Coding

Communication

Welcome!

How can I find my way around school?

1 Look, read and number.

Art _____ •—

PE _____ •—

—• Science _____

—• Maths _____

2 Look at the timetable. Which two days are the same?

CODE CRACKER

Monday	Tuesday	Wednesday	Thursday	Friday
÷ +	🧪	✏️	÷ +	🧪
🧪	⚽	⚽	🧪	⚽
🍴	🍴	🍴	✏️	🍴
⚽	÷ +	÷ +	🍴	÷ +
✏️	✏️	🧪	⚽	✏️

3 Listen and circle.

Come in, sit down; welcome everyone!

It's the end of a long day,

Time to have fun / lunch and play!

Max, Yara and Freddie,

Nadir and Ellie – all ready!

Read, do Maths / Art , do your Maths / Science homework, too.

There's lots to do for me and you!

Welcome everyone!

 I can find my way around school.

My school

VOCABULARY

I will learn school subjects and places.

1 Look and write.

1 _____

2 _____

3 _____

2 Which is Max's school? Tick ☑.

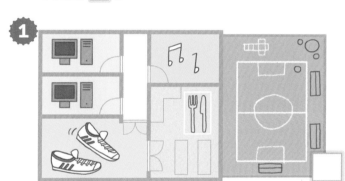

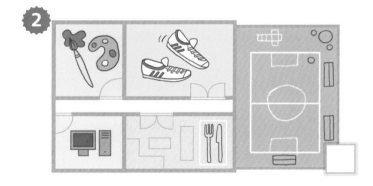

3 Read and answer. Compare with a partner.

Where do you do it?

What's your favourite subject?

4 Look, listen and write.

English   Geography   History

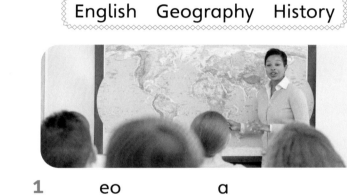

1 _____eo_____ _____a_____ _____ _____

attend
medieval
secondary school
borrow

2 E_____ _____ _____i_____ _____

3 _____i_____ _____o_____ _____

School rules

LANGUAGE LAB

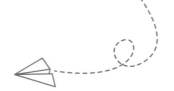

I will talk about classroom rules.

1 Write the words in order.

1 eat / in / Don't / class / .

   Don't eat in class.

2 to / other / each / Listen / .

   _____

3 late / Don't / be / .

   _____

4 toys / into / class / bring / Don't / .

   _____

5 books / your / remember / Always / .

   _____

6 and / hard / fun / Work / have / !

   _____

2 Look and write the rules.

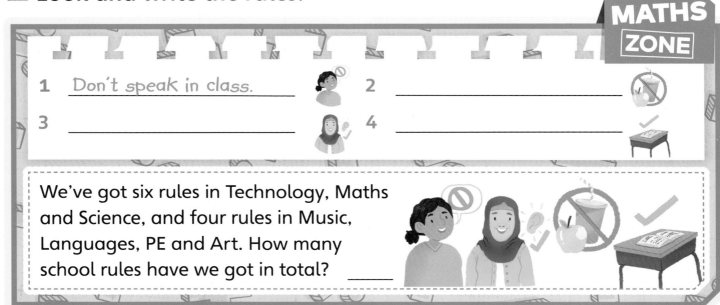

MATHS ZONE

1 *Don't speak in class.*

2 _____

3 _____

4 _____

We've got six rules in Technology, Maths and Science, and four rules in Music, Languages, PE and Art. How many school rules have we got in total? _____

3 Where do you hear these instructions? Write S (School), H (Home) or B (Both).

1 Put your hand up to speak. _____

2 Switch off the TV. _____

3 Have a shower. _____

4 Don't be late. _____

I can talk about classroom rules.

Story lab

READING

1 Look and label.

Ellie   Freddie   Max   Nadir   Yara

2 Read. Circle T (True) or F (False).

1   It's Yara's first day at school.   T / F

2   Ellie loses her jacket.   T / F

3   It's Tuesday.   T / F

4   Yara goes to the gym.   T / F

3 Complete the instructions from the story. Match. You can use a character more than once.

Don't go   Look   Put   Take

1   _____ so fast!

2   _____ your jacket and your bag here.

3   _____ your jacket off!

4   _____ in the art room.

I can read a story and learn about school.

1 Show time!

How can I make a flip book?

1 Read and match.

1 juggle

2 do magic tricks

3 play computer games

2 Look, read and number.

CODE CRACKER

1

2

3

Taylor can dance but can't juggle or sing. _____

Lee can't sing or juggle but can play computer games. _____

Riley can juggle and dance but can't do magic tricks. _____

3 Listen and circle.

It's show time, it's show time!

Everyone's on the stage.

There are a lot of children,

Boys and girls of every age.

Can you act / sing ? Can you dance / sing ?

You can do anything!

It's show time, it's show time!

Everyone's together.

Fred is doing a magic show,

His tricks are really clever!

Can you clap your hands / spin around ? Can you do gymnastics / play computer games , too?

Let's put on a show for me and you!

I can talk about actions and performances.

What can we do?

VOCABULARY

I will learn action words.

1 Order the letters and write the words.

1   tesp to the ised   _____

2   vwae   _____

3   ggulej   _____

4   setp wrsdackba   _____

5   do whcaelesrt   _____

6   mapst   _____

7   ptes worfsdar   _____

8   do ticsnasgym   _____

9   psin oundar   _____

10   plac   _____

11   tac   _____

12   do gicam scktri   _____

2 🎧 006 Listen to the children. Tick ☑ or cross ☒.

	Juggle	Do magic tricks	Do cartwheels	Act
Shemina				
Justin				
Chen				

3 Do your own class survey. Then ask and answer and record your results.

Can you do gymnastics?

Yes, I can.

EXTRA VOCABULARY

4 🎧 007 Look and write. Then listen and check.

ballet
ballroom dancing
hip-hop
tap dancing

_____   _____   _____   _____

 **I know** action words.

Language lab 1

GRAMMAR: WHAT ARE YOU / HE / SHE / THEY DOING?

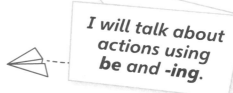

I will talk about actions using **be** and **-ing**.

1 **Complete with the correct form of the action words.**

1 What _____ Etta _____ (do)? She _____ (spin) around.

2 Luis _____ (not wave) his arms, he _____ (clap) his hands!

3 _____ they _____ (step) backwards? No, _____ .

4 What _____ you _____ (do)? I _____ (stamp) my foot.

5 Katie _____ (juggle), she _____ (not do) magic tricks.

2 **Which picture matches the sentences in 1? Look and circle _a_ or _b_.**

3 **Write about picture _a_.**

1 Etta _____ (+)

2 Luis _____ (?)

3 They _____ (-)

4 You _____ (?)

5 Katie _____ (+)

4 🛠 Make a dancing person. Move it and say.

What is she doing?

She's stepping backwards.

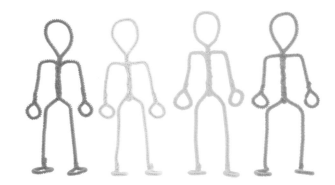

5 🎧 008 Listen and tick ☑.

1

a  ☐

b  ☐

2

a  ☐

b  ☐

3

a  ☐

b  ☐

4

a  ☐

b  ☐

6 Imagine it's Saturday at 11 a.m. Write a message saying what you are doing.

Hi! What are you doing?

11:00

7 💬 Ask and answer. Find someone who has got the same activity as you.

Are you playing computer games?

No, I'm not.

I can talk about action words using be and -ing .

Story lab

READING

I will read a story about a talent show.

1 Complete the sentences. Then match.

a Freddie's doing magic tricks very well!

My turn!

b I'm drawing.

c No, I don't like shows. I can't sing or act or anything.

d What are you doing, Ellie?

I'm getting ready for the talent show.

e Yes, and Max's doing gymnastics. It's a great routine!

f What's Ellie doing?

1 _____ _____ getting ready for the _____ _____ ?

2 She _____ _____ computer games. She doesn't like shows.

3 Look at Max! He's _____ _____ really well! What _____ you _____ ?

4 No, _____ _____ . You _____ taking _____ .

5 Wow! Yara's _____ well! She _____ dropping anything!

6 And Snowball _____ _____ away!

2 Read the story again. Circle T (True) or F (False).

1 Ellie doesn't like talent shows. **T / F**

2 Ellie isn't drawing. **T / F**

3 Yara is doing gymnastics. **T / F**

4 Ellie performs her talent. **T / F**

3 Look at the different endings for the story and complete.

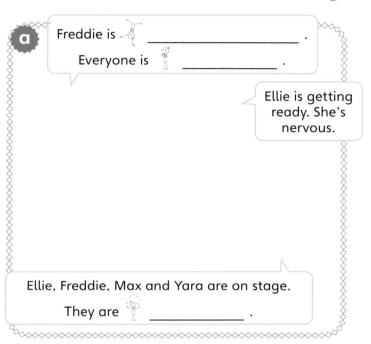

a Freddie is _____ .

Everyone is _____ .

Ellie is getting ready. She's nervous.

Ellie, Freddie, Max and Yara are on stage.

They are _____ .

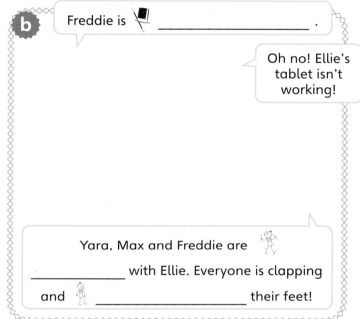

b Freddie is _____ .

Oh no! Ellie's tablet isn't working!

Yara, Max and Freddie are _____ with Ellie. Everyone is clapping and _____ their feet!

4 Draw one of the frames from 3. Show a partner. Can they guess which one?

5 Think about the story. Answer.

1 Whose talent do you like?

_____

2 Imagine you are in the show. What's your talent? _____

3 Imagine you are going on stage. How do you feel? _____

6 Make your story book.
→ page 115

→ page 115

I can read a story about a talent show.

Phonics lab

I will learn the **a**, **e** and **i** sounds.

1 🎧 009 Listen and tick ☑ . Then say.

1

2

3

4

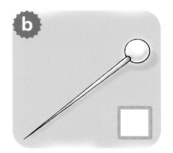

2 Choose and write six words. Play *Bingo*!

bin

clap

dance

man

men

pet

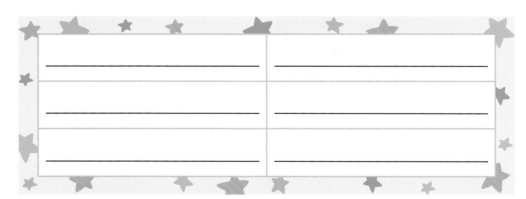

sing

snap

spin

step

twin

left

3 🎧 010 Listen and say the tongue twister. Then listen again and write.

_____

_____

I know the **a**, **e** and **i** sounds.

Experiment lab

I will learn about bones and muscles.

1 Read, match and complete.

1 She's singing. She's using muscles in her ___chest___ and _____ . ☐

2 He's sitting up. He's using muscles in his _____ . ☐

FACE

CHEST

STOMACH

2 Read the fun facts and circle. Then listen and check.

There are 26 / 206 / 2600 bones in the human body.

The heart is a bone / muscle .

Babies / Adults have got more bones.

A / uses more muscles.

EXPERIMENT TIME

Report

1 **Think about your experiment. Read and answer.**

1 Which pose was easy?

2 Which pose was difficult?

3 Which muscles do you feel when you do the poses?

2 **Write your report.**

Yoga moves

The tree was easy. When I do this pose, I'm using muscles in my ...

I know about bones and muscles.

Language lab 2

GRAMMAR: DESCRIBING ACTIONS

I will describe actions using well / quickly / badly.

1 🎧 012 What's happening now? Listen and tick ☑.

1

a

b

2

a

b

3

a

b

4

a

b

2 Change the words to describe actions. Then say a sentence.

1 good   _____

2 bad   _____

3 quick   _____

4 slow   _____

5 beautiful   _____

6 backwards   _____

3 ⬭ Play *Two True, One False*.

I dance beautifully. I run quickly. I juggle well.

'I run quickly' is false!

No – try again!

I can describe actions using well / quickly / badly .

What are we doing?

COMMUNICATION

I will talk about what my friends are doing.

1 013 **Listen and write.**

Monday   Tuesday   Wednesday   Thursday

_____

_____

_____

_____

2 Think of your school week. Write what you are doing each day.

Monday	Tuesday	Wednesday	Thursday	Friday
2 p.m.	10 p.m.	11:30 p.m.	1:30 p.m.	12 p.m.
_____	_____	_____	_____	_____
_____	_____	_____	_____	_____

3 Work with a partner. Take turns to say what you are doing. Guess the time and the day.

I can talk about what my friends are doing.

19

Make a flip book

1 What routine is in your flip book? Tick ☑ or cross ☒.

Dance ☐ 　　Magic tricks ☐ 　　Other: _____

Gymnastics ☐ 　　Juggling ☐

2 Complete your project report.

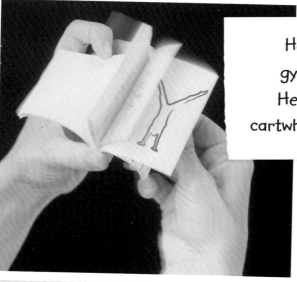

He's doing gymnastics. He's doing a cartwheel very well!

She's dancing. She's clapping her hands quickly and stepping to the side.

3 💬 Present your flip book to your family and friends.

4 Think about your project and colour.

I can make a flip book.

5 Work with a partner. Look at the frames from the story. Say what's happening. Guess the frame.

They are doing magic tricks. Snowball isn't running away.

Frame 7!

6 Which character is it? Listen, find and write.

_____ _____ _____ _____ _____

7 Read and answer.

1   What do you do well? _____

2   What do you do badly? _____

3   Imagine you can do any talent well. What is it? _____

4   What is your favourite dance move? _____

2 Frozen

How can I create a museum exhibition?

1 Label the pictures.

tail trunk tusks wings

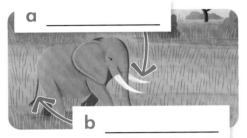
a _____
b _____

c _____

d _____

2 Look and read. Circle T (True) or F (False).

CODE CRACKER

a It's got a trunk and wings. T / F

b It's got a trunk or wings. T / F

c It's got a trunk not a tail. T / F

3 ⚙ 015 Listen and match.

The Ice Age was a long time ago.

1 The Ice Age was full of ice and snow!

2 Ice Age animals were big and hairy.

3 Some were cute and cuddly and others very scary!

There were woolly mammoths, sabre-toothed tigers, too.

4 And scary, hairy humans a bit like me and you!

I can talk about the Ice Age.

Describing the Ice Age

VOCABULARY

I will learn weather and animal words.

1 Look and circle.

1 hairy / tail   2 cloudy / sunny

3 icy / windy   4 tusks / trunk

5 cold / warm   6 rainy / snowy

2 016 Listen to the children. Number the pictures.

3 Play the *Description Game* in pairs.

EXTRA VOCABULARY

4 017 Look and label. Then listen and check.

hail   heatwave
hurricane   thunderstorm

1 t_____   2 h_____

3 h_____   4 h_____

I know weather and animal words.

Language lab 1

GRAMMAR: IT WAS / WAS NOT …

I will talk about the past.

1 Read and circle.

1   The weather in the Ice Age was / were cold and snowy.

2   Ice Age animals was / were very big and hairy.

3   It wasn't / weren't warm in the Ice Age.

4   I 'm not / wasn't alive in the Ice Age.

5   Is / Were woolly mammoths bigger than elephants?

6   They wasn't / weren't at the museum yesterday.

2 Rewrite the sentences so they are about the past.

1   The mammoth is big.

_____

2   We aren't at school.

_____

3   Is it snowy? Yes, it is.

_____

4   I'm not warm.

_____

5   The mammoth is hairy.

_____

6   The lake is icy.

_____

3 Match the sentences from 2 to the pictures. Number.

a   Sentence numbers:

_____ _____ _____

b   Sentence numbers:

_____ _____ _____

4 ⚙ 018 Listen and complete.

1 Jo **2** Corin **3** Leo **4** Kim **5** Sarah **6** Novak

Find someone who was ...

Activity	Name	Activity	Name
ⓐ ... asleep at 6:30 this morning.		ⓔ ... at home on Saturday afternoon.	
ⓑ ... on holiday in August.		ⓕ ... in the shower at 7:00 this morning.	
ⓒ ... in bed at 9:00 last night.		ⓖ ... at the park after school yesterday.	
ⓓ ... happy yesterday.		ⓗ ... at a restaurant last night.	

5 💬 Play *Find Someone Who* ... Use the ideas from 4 and add your own.

> Were you in the shower at seven o'clock?

> No, I wasn't. I was on the school bus.

6 Answer the questions. Use full sentences.

Where were you on Saturday?

Who were you with?

What was the weather like?

I can talk about the past.

Story lab

The museum scare

1 🎧 019 **Number the story frames in order. Then listen and check.**

2 💬 **Retell the story in pairs.**

Can you spot me in every frame?

26

3 Complete the speech bubbles with the past of be. Which frame are they from? Number.

a

What _____ that?!

There _____ two hairy ears. It was the bear – it's following me!

What?

b

Wow! There _____ big, scary bears in the Ice Age.

Their hair _____ really thick.

c

Phew! It _____ (not) a bear!

It _____ a little kid.

d

What _____ that noise?

It _____ the bear. It's alive!

4  Listen and circle.

1

2

3

5 Think about the story. Read and answer.

1 Was Yara's joke funny? _____

2 Who was scared? _____

3 What was in the museum? _____

4 Imagine you are Freddie or Yara in Frame 6. How do you feel? _____

6 Write a new ending. ➡ page 123

I can read a story about a museum.

Phonics lab

*I will learn the **o** and **u** sounds.*

1 🎧 021 Listen and tick ☑. Then say.

1 **a**

b

2 **a**

b

3 **a**

b

2 🎧 022 Listen and number in order. Then chant.

3 ✏ Choose words. Make your own chant.

box   dog   duck   fox   hop   jog   jug   run   trunk   tusk

_____

_____

_____

I know the **o** and **u** sounds.

Experiment lab

I will learn about fossils.

1 Read about fossils again. Then circle.

1 A fossil is an animal that was alive last week / a long time ago .

2 An ammonite / A sabre-toothed tiger was a sea animal.

3 Insects / Fossils can be rocks and bones.

4 Footprints / Skeletons are bone fossils.

2 Draw arrows to the timeline.

MATHS ZONE

475 million years old

325 million years old

250 million years old

75 million years old

500
400
300
200
100
0

EXPERIMENT TIME

Report

1 Which method did you use? Tick ☑ . Compare your results with other groups.

warm water ☐   salt ☐

metal spoon ☐

2 Think about your experiment and circle.

After being in ice, my fossil was the same / different .

I think the Ice Age ended because of force 🔨 / heat 🔥 / salt 🧂 .

3 Write your report.

FOSSILS IN ICE

Warm water was fast – 2 minutes, 33 seconds.

Language lab 2

GRAMMAR: THERE WAS / THERE WERE

I will compare then and now.

1 Read and complete. Use the correct form of there + be.

●●●

PANGEA

Today **1** _____ seven continents, but about 300 million

years ago **2** _____ just one huge continent called Pangea.

3 _____ just one huge sea called Panthalassa. The weather on

Pangea was hot and sunny, but **4** _____ rainy seasons.

5 _____ life on Pangea. **6** _____ a lot of insects and

7 _____ the first dinosaurs. **8** _____ (not) any humans!

9 _____ only a few fossils from the Panthalassa sea today, but we

know **10** _____ ammonites, coral and sharks in the sea.

2 Read again and write short answers.

1   Were there seven continents 300 million years ago?   _____

2   Was there one huge sea?   _____

3   Was there an Ice Age on Pangea?   _____

4   Were there insects?   _____

5   Were there humans?   _____

6   Was there life in the sea?   _____

3 Play *Kim's Game*.

Was there a pencil?

No, there wasn't. There were two pens.

I can compare now and then.

What's the weather?

COMMUNICATION

I will describe the weather.

1 🎧 023 Listen and write.

Beijing   Krakow   Mexico City   Moscow

☀️ 21°	☁️🌧️ 19°	☁️❄️ -3°	☁️ 2°
Name of place:	Name of place:	Name of place:	Name of place:
1 _____	2 _____	3 _____	4 _____

2 Write what the weather was like for three of the days.

Monday	Tuesday	Wednesday	Thursday	Friday	Saturday	Sunday
☀️🌬️ 20°	🌧️ 6°	☀️☁️❄️ 0°	☁️❄️🌬️ 3°	🌧️ 22°	☀️🌬️ 2°	☁️❄️ 2°

It was sunny, icy and cold. _____   _____

_____   _____

3 💬 💡 Work with a partner. Take turns to read your weather descriptions and guess the day.

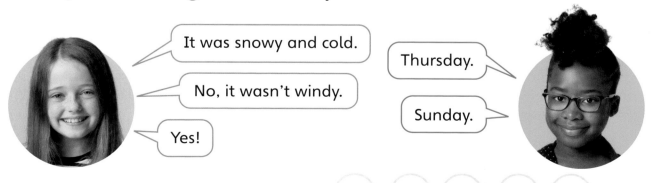

It was snowy and cold.

Thursday.

No, it wasn't windy.

Sunday.

Yes!

I can describe the weather.

Create a mini museum exhibition

Project report

1 What was in your museum exhibition? Tick .

Skeletons ☐   Sabre-toothed tigers ☐

Fossils ☐   Other: _____

Woolly mammoths ☐

2 Complete your project report.

Our exhibition was good. There were two woolly mammoths. There was a sabre-toothed tiger skeleton and there were three insect fossils. The weather was snowy and sunny.

3 💬 Present your report to your family and friends.

This is my museum exhibition. There are two bears.

4 Think about your project and colour.

I can create a mini museum exhibition.

5 Describe an animal from the unit for a partner to guess.

It's got a tail. It's got a trunk.

No. It's hairy.

Yes!

Elephant?

Woolly mammoth!

6 Complete with the correct form of be.

1 It _____ a very sunny day yesterday, but it _____ (not) warm!

2 There _____ a lot of interesting fossils in the museum yesterday.

3 There _____ (not) any dinosaurs in the Ice Age.

4 My brother _____ at home last night.

5 They _____ (not) at the museum yesterday.

6 What _____ the weather like in the Ice Age?

7 Read and answer.

1 What was your favourite animal in the unit? _____

2 What was your favourite museum exhibit? _____

3 What's your favourite weather? _____

4 What was your favourite story frame? _____

Now go to your Progress Chart on page 4.

1 Checkpoint

1 Listen. Write Y (Yesterday), M (Morning) or N (Now).

a   It was sunny.   T / F

b   He's stepping
    backwards.   T / F

c   He's doing
    magic tricks.   T / F

2 Look at 1 again. Read and circle T (True) or F (False).

3 Draw paths. Then write.

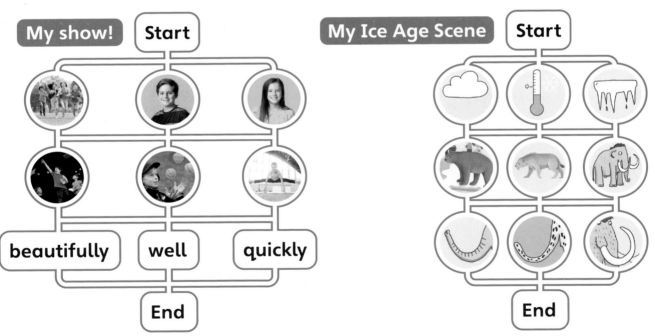

They were juggling quickly.

It was icy. There was a bear.
There wasn't a trunk.

_____

4 Compare sentences from 3 with a partner. Trace their path.

Traditions

1 Read about Spain again. Complete.

1 Spain is in the continent of _____ .

2 The climate in the south of Spain is _____ .

3 The population of Spain is more than _____ .

2 025 Listen and match.

1 Liam _____

2 Faiza _____

3 Ignacio _____

3 Imagine you're in Spain. Look at the picture and complete the postcard to a family member.

Hi _____ !

1 I'm in _____ . It's _____ .

2 I'm _____ .

3 They're _____ .

They're _____ .

4 We're having a _____ time!

Lots of love,

_____

Say where you are and what the weather is like.

Use the picture. Say what you are doing.

Describe what the people in the picture are doing.

Give your opinion of the holiday.

3 Celebrations!

How can I create a festival parade?

1 Complete the sentences.

exciting   happy   noisy   relaxing

1 I'm reading in bed.
   It's _____ .

2 I'm with my family.
   I feel _____ .

3 I'm at a festival.
   It's really _____ .

4 I'm at a football match.
   It's really _____ .

2 Choose two words from 1. Tell a partner about an experience.

My birthday party was exciting. I was happy.

3 What's next? Look and complete.

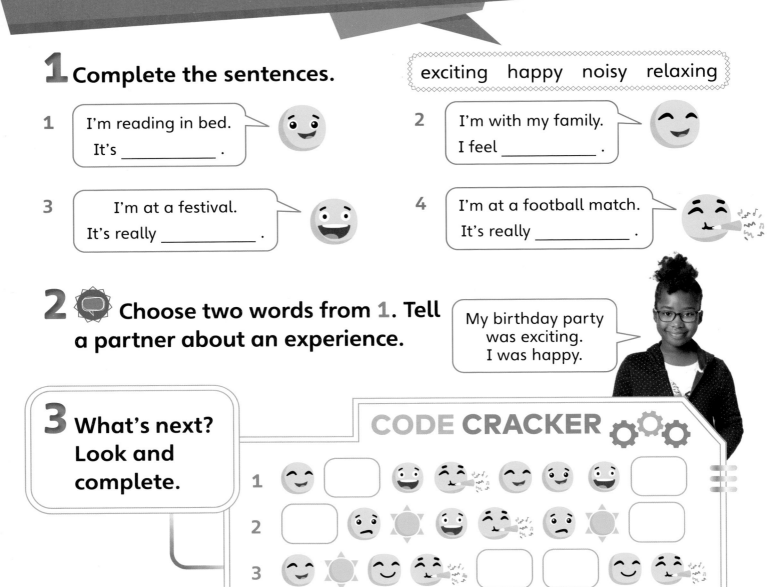

CODE CRACKER

4 Listen, read and circle.

1 The song is about a basketball match / festival .

2 The festival is noisy / quiet .

3 The festival is big / small .

I can talk about celebrations.

Describing things

VOCABULARY

I will learn describing words.

1 Look and match for you.

boring
colourful
disgusting
exciting
fun
hungry

interesting
noisy
quiet
relaxing
tasty
thirsty

2 What numbers are missing? Look and complete.

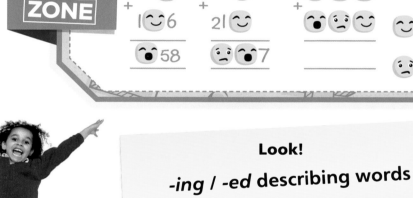

MATHS ZONE

23 + 1⌣6 = ⌣58

32 + 21 = ⌣7

3 Role-play the words in 1 for your partner to guess.

Fun? — No.
Exciting? — Yes!

EXTRA VOCABULARY

Look!

-ing / *-ed* describing words

It is exciting. → describes an event

She is excited. → describes how a person feels

4 Look and label. Then listen and check.

1 fireworks _____   2 float _____   3 lanterns _____   4 parade _____

a

b

c

d

 **I know** describing words.

Language lab 1

GRAMMAR: IT'S MORE ...

I will learn to describe events.

1 Read and circle.

1 Fireworks are more noisy / noisier than lanterns.

2 Going to a festival is more good / better fun than staying at home.

3 My clothes are more colourful / more better than my mum's clothes.

4 Our town festival is more small / smaller this year.

5 I'm happier / more happy today than yesterday.

6 This book is more exciting / thirstier than that book.

2 Write sentences about the pictures.

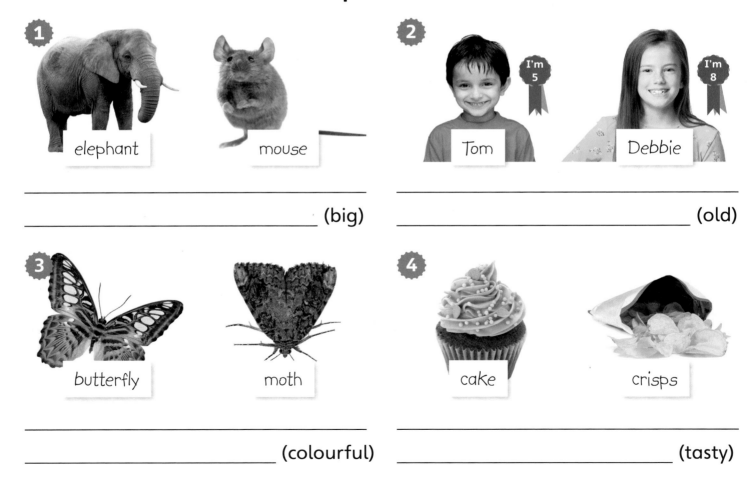

1 elephant   mouse

_____
_____ (big)

2 Tom   I'm 5   Debbie   I'm 8

_____
_____ (old)

3 butterfly   moth

_____
_____ (colourful)

4 cake   crisps

_____
_____ (tasty)

3  Write the names of two friends. Think of sentences to describe them. Use the words.

> colourful (clothes)   long (hair)   old   short (hair)   small   tall   young

_____   _____

> Ana has got longer hair than Rafa.

> Rafa is taller than Ana.

Look!

has got + longer + hair + than

is + taller + than

4 Listen and circle Jake's bag.

a
b
c
d
e

5 Write three sentences comparing the bags.

1   The black bag is _____ .

2   _____

3   _____

6 Read your sentences to a partner. Find someone who wrote the same sentences as you.

> The black bag is bigger than the pink bag.

> I've got 'The black bag is bigger than the pink bag', too!

I can   describe events.

Story lab

READING

I will read a story about festivals.

Castletown parade

1 🔊 029 **Match and number the speech bubbles. Then listen and check.**

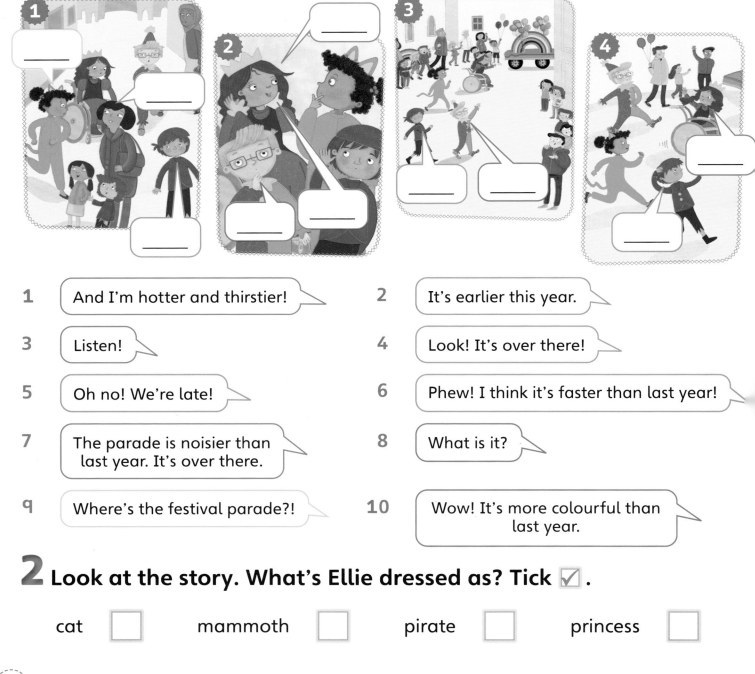

1	And I'm hotter and thirstier!	**2**	It's earlier this year.
3	Listen!	**4**	Look! It's over there!
5	Oh no! We're late!	**6**	Phew! I think it's faster than last year!
7	The parade is noisier than last year. It's over there.	**8**	What is it?
9	Where's the festival parade?!	**10**	Wow! It's more colourful than last year.

2 Look at the story. What's Ellie dressed as? Tick ☑.

cat ☐   mammoth ☐   pirate ☐   princess ☐

40

3 Read and circle T (True) or F (False).

1   The parade was later last year.   T / F

2   The parade was more colourful last year.   T / F

3   The parade is faster this year.   T / F

4   Yara is hotter this year.   T / F

5   The food is disgusting.   T / F

4 Look. Write sentences to compare the characters.

Yara is happier than Max.

_____

_____

_____

5 Make stick puppets of the characters.

Draw and colour in the story characters.

Cut out.

Stick on a lollipop stick.

6   Act out the story with your stick puppets.

7 Make your own story book. page 117

I can read a story about festivals.

Phonics lab

I will learn **a_e** and **i_e**.

1 🎧 030 Write. Then listen, check and say.

bike   cage   cake   five   game   kite   name   rice

1 _____

2 _____

3 _____

4 _____

5 _____

6 _____

7 _____

8 _____

2 🎧 031 Listen and number the pictures.

1 We're late for the parade.

2 I hate to be late!

3 There are games at the parade.

4 And there's cake!

5 Ride your bike.

6 Fly your kite.

7 Eat some rice.

8 High five! That's nice!

3 Listen again and chant in groups. One group chants a_e words, the other group chants i_e words.

I know the **a_e** and **i_e** sounds.

Experiment lab

I will learn about symmetry.

1 032 **Which mask is Gianni's? Tick ☑ .**

1 ☐

2 ☐

3 ☐

4 ☐

2 **Colour and complete the masks.**

1

Repeating pattern

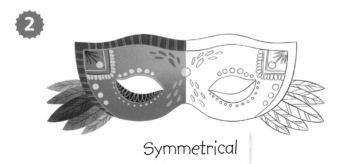

2

Symmetrical

EXPERIMENT TIME

Report

1 Think about your experiment. Complete and then compare with a partner.

1 Which picture was more colourful?

_____

2 Which picture was more beautiful?

_____

3 Which was easier to create?

_____

2 Write your report.

My first picture was more colourful and more beautiful. It was easier to make.

 **I know** about symmetry.

43

Language lab 2

GRAMMAR: BEST, WORST, MOST EXCITING …

I will learn to compare things using -est / most.

1 Listen to Greg talking about his hobbies. Then match.

playing drums

yoga

cooking

- exciting
- good
- tasty
- noisy
- relaxing
- quiet

2 Read and complete the information.

CODE CRACKER

Park School, Castle School and Oak School have floats in the festival parade. The three themes are animals, films and cities. The floats are 5, 7 and 8 metres long. They are 6, 9 and 10 metres high. Use the clues to work out the theme, the length and the height of each school's float.

- Park School's float is 10 metres high.
- Castle School's float isn't the longest or the shortest.
- Oak School's float is 4 metres shorter in height than Park School's.
- Castle School's float isn't the city theme.
- The animal theme float is 7 metres long.
- The city theme float is the tallest.
- The film theme float is the longest.

	length	height	theme
Oak School			
Castle School			
Park School			

I can compare things using -est / most .

Giving opinions

COMMUNICATION

I will learn to give my opinion.

1 Listen to the book club. Which book do they all like the best?

WONDER

The story of a boy with a different face starting school.

_____

_____

charlie and the chocolate Factory

The most incredible adventure of a boy and an exciting chocolate factory.

_____

_____

_____

_____

PIPPI LONGSTOCKING

Pippi is the strongest girl in the world. She has the craziest adventures with her friends.

_____

_____

_____

2 Listen again. Write the words to describe each book.

amazing   bad   boring   funny   exciting   good   interesting   sad

3 Do you agree or disagree with each statement? Write your opinion, then compare with a partner.

1   I think festivals are boring. _____

2   I think books are more interesting than films. _____

3   I think warm, sunny weather is better than cold, snowy weather.

_____

4   I think school is exciting. _____

I can give my opinion.

Create a festival parade

Project report

1 Complete the sentences about your festival parade.

We made: _____

The most colourful thing is: _____

One item with a repeating pattern is: _____

One item with a symmetrical pattern is: _____

2 Complete your project report.

We've got an animal theme.
It's the most colourful parade.
We've got symmetrical masks
and feather headdresses.
We are beautiful birds.

3 Present your report to your family and friends.

This is our festival parade. We've got colourful masks. It was the noisiest parade!

4 Think about your project and colour.

I can create a festival parade.

5 Talk about festivals with a partner. Agree and disagree.

Lantern Festival

Rio Carnival

Kite Festival

Holi Festival

> I think the Rio Carnival is the most exciting.

> I disagree. I think Holi festival is more exciting.

6 Order the words to make sentences.

1 is / town's / the / boring / festival / world / the / Our / most / festival / in / !

_____

2 week / is / exciting / than / more / a / Carnival / week / normal / .

_____

3 tastier / food / last / The / year / than / is / .

_____

4 noisy / the / you / Do / best / like / festivals / ?

_____

7 Read and answer.

1 What was your favourite festival in the unit?

_____

2 Which of your friends do you agree with the most?

_____

3 What was your favourite story frame?

_____

4 Blast off!

How can I create a puppet space journey?

1 Label the pictures.

1
w _____

2
t _____

3
e _____

4
b _____

5
w _____

2 Read the instructions. What's the problem? Correct.

CODE CRACKER

Start → Start putting fuel in rocket → Get in rocket → Launch rocket → End

3 Listen and match.

035

1 We launched the rocket to the Moon.
   Goodbye Earth, see you soon! ●

2 We walked on the Moon in white space suits. ●

3 We floated in our big space boots.
   We are coming home soon. ●

4 Wave goodbye to the silver Moon. ●

I can talk about space.

What's in space?

VOCABULARY

I will learn space words.

1 Read and match. What space words on page 58 of the Pupil's Book are missing?

a launch

b satellite

c study

d astronaut

e rocket

f space

g float

h live

i space station

EXTRA VOCABULARY

2 036 Listen and match.

1 Bill   2 Rona   3 Tariq

3 037 Look and label. Then listen and check.

Earth _____   Jupiter _____   Neptune _____
Mercury _____   Saturn _____

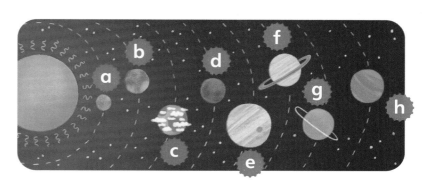

I **know** space words.

Language lab 1

GRAMMAR: HE / SHE _____... -ED.

I will learn to talk about the past using -ed.

1 Complete the sentences with the past of the action words. Read the article again and circle T (True) or F (False).

1 She _____ (start) studying at Stanford University when she was 18.   T / F

2 Mae Jemison _____ (study) engineering at Cornell University.   T / F

3 She _____ (not study) medicine.   T / F

4 She _____ (work) as a doctor in Africa and the United States.   T / F

5 She _____ (travel) in space in 1992.   T / F

2 🎧 038 Listen to information about four astronauts. Complete the sentences.

SPACE RECORD BREAKERS

1 Sally Ride _____ to space twice.

2 Valeri Polyakov _____ in space for more than 14 months.

3 Guion Bluford _____ Aerospace Engineering.

4 Anne McClain and Christina Koch _____ in space together.

3 Rewrite the sentences in the negative form.

1 She travelled around the Earth.

_____

2 They worked on the space station.

_____

3 We launched the rocket.

_____

4 He breathed with an oxygen pack.

_____

4 Listen to the three pronunciations of -ed. Sort the words.

worked
started
launched
rained

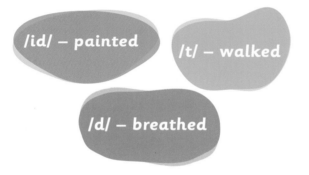

/id/ – painted

/t/ – walked

/d/ – breathed

floated
looked
lived
visited
studied

5 Find the way to the Moon. You can only go on /id/ endings.

CODE CRACKER

started	lived	landed	travelled	walked
worked	wanted	rained	visited	finished
studied	launched	liked	breathed	floated

Story lab

READING

SPACE TRIP

1 🎧 040 **Listen and number in order. Then match.**

a   The rocket landed and we walked on the Moon!   _____

b   Then the rocket launched and we blasted into space!   _____

c   We entered a space rocket …   _____

d   We floated – it was amazing!   _____

e   We landed back on Earth.   _____

f   We opened the rocket door and here we are!   _____

g   What happened next?   _____

h   Where did you go? A space station?   _____

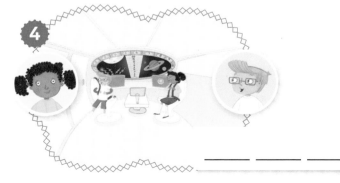

2 💬 **Retell the story in pairs.**

3 **Read and circle T (True) or F (False).**

1   Yara and Freddie were in a space simulator.   T / F

2   Ellie and Max travelled to a space station in the simulator.   T / F

3   They walked on the Moon in the simulator.   T / F

4   They were in the simulator for 15 minutes.   T / F

5   Everyone else wanted to go in the simulator.   T / F

4 ⚙️ **Think of a simulator experience. Draw and write.**

In my simulator, I visited …
I liked …
I didn't like …

5 💬 **Describe 4 to a partner. Compare.**

The rocket launched. I travelled to a space station. I walked in space.

6 ⚙️ **Write a new ending.**
   ➡️ **page 124**

I can read a story about a space trip.

Phonics lab

O_E AND U_E

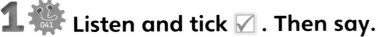

I will learn the **long o** and **long u** sounds.

1 🎧 041 Listen and tick ☑ . Then say.

1 **a** cone ☐

b cube ☐

2 **a** tune ☐

b stone ☐

3 **a** nose ☐

b huge ☐

2 🎧 042 Listen and say the chant again. Then circle the words with o_e and underline the words with u_e.

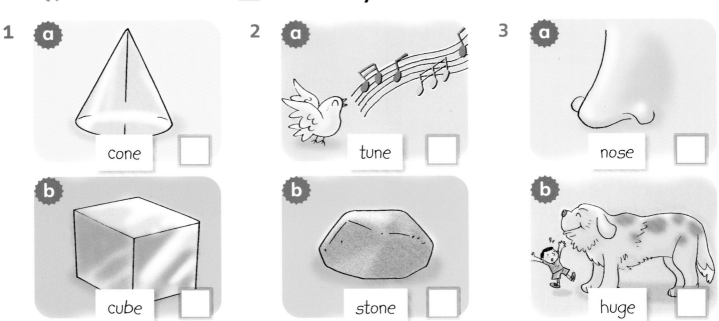

I travelled around the globe

On a huge space probe.

I landed on a stone.

I talked on my phone.

Look! My cute home.

3 Complete the tongue twister. Then say.

There was a  _____ , a △ _____ and a 📱 _____

in my 🏠 _____ .

I know the long **o** and **u** sounds.

Experiment lab

TECHNOLOGY: ROCKETS

1 Read the fun facts and circle. Then listen and check.

1 A rocket launches at 8 (kilometres) / metres per second.

2 The fastest ever spacecraft travelled at 356 / 356,000 kilometres per hour.

3 Space starts at 100 / 1000 kilometres above Earth.

4 The average journey time for a space shuttle from Earth to space is around 8 / 80 minutes.

5 The Moon is a natural rocket / satellite going around Earth.

2 Read and answer.

MATHS ZONE

1 How far does a rocket launched at 8 km/second travel in one minute? _____

2 How far does a rocket travelling 356,000 km/h go in a day? _____

EXPERIMENT TIME

Report

1 Think about your experiment. Answer, then compare with a partner.

1 Which method was the best? Why?

_____

2 Which method didn't work?

_____

3 Imagine you use six tablets. What happens?

_____

2 Write your report.

Rockets

My first rocket was the fastest. I used ...

My second rocket was the fastest. I used ...

Language lab 2

GRAMMAR: DID HE / SHE ...?

1 Read and number the pictures in order.

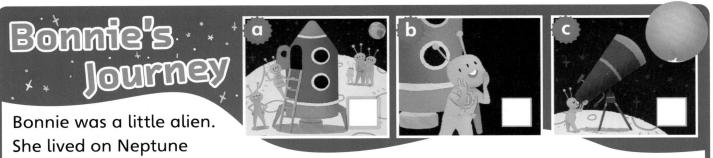

Bonnie's Journey

Bonnie was a little alien. She lived on Neptune with her mum, dad and brother. One night, she looked through her telescope and looked at Earth. She dreamt of travelling to Earth. One day she visited her friend, Jammy, and she talked to him about Earth. Jammy invented a rocket for Bonnie. They launched the rocket on Bonnie's birthday – she was 10. When she arrived on Earth, she was 12! She landed in the Rio de Janeiro Carnival. She looked around – she was ready for an adventure!

2 Read again. Look at the answers and write the questions.

1 _____ look at through her telescope? Earth.

2 Who _____ ? Her friend, Jammy.

3 When _____ ? On her birthday.

4 _____ ? In the Rio de Janeiro Carnival.

3 ⚙ Use the words to write your own alien story.

> dream float land launch like live
> look start travel visit walk want

Once upon a time there was a little alien called ...

4 💬 Read your story to a partner. Ask and answer questions.

I can ask about the past using Did he / she ...?

I like to …

COMMUNICATION

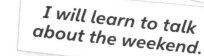

I will learn to talk about the weekend.

1 🎧 044 Listen and number the projects in order.

 a

b

 c

d

 e

2 💬 Play a game. Choose a project from 1. Ask and answer with a partner to guess.

Did you paint a rocket?

Yes, I did.

Picture 4!

3 💬 Do a class weekend survey. Think of six activities. Ask the class.

Watched TV |||| |||| |
Walked in the park |||| |||| ||||
Played on a tablet |||| |||| |||| |||

Did you watch TV?

Yes, I did.

Did you walk in the park?

No, I didn't.

4 What activity is most popular in your class?

 I can talk about the weekend.

57

PROJECT AND REVIEW UNIT 4

Create a puppet space journey

Project report

1 Think of your astronaut. Read and answer.

Did he/she ...

... walk on the Moon?

_____

... travel to the ISS?

_____

... walk in space?

_____

... study aerospace engineering?

_____

... work on a space station?

_____

Other: _____

2 Complete your project report.

The rocket launched and travelled to Venus. The astronaut walked on Venus.

3 Present your report to your family and friends.

This is my puppet of Neil Armstrong. He travelled to the Moon and walked on the Moon.

4 Think about your project and colour.

I can create a puppet space journey.

5 Read and answer about this unit.

PUPIL'S BOOK

1 Who entered the space simulator in the story? _____

2 Where did Chris Hadfield play the guitar? _____

3 When did Mae Jemison travel in space? _____

4 Did Mae Jemison visit the Moon? _____

5 Who was the first person to use Spanish in space? _____

ACTIVITY BOOK

6 Which planet is closest to the Sun? _____

7 Which astronauts walked in space together in October 2019? _____

8 Did Valeri Polyakov live in space for more than 14 months? _____

9 Where did the alien called Bonnie live? _____

10 Where did Bonnie's rocket land? _____

6 Use the pictures to write a story.

The rocket launched from _____

1  Listen. Where are they? Tick ☑.

At a festival ☐   At a space museum ☐

2 💡 Read and circle the odd one out.

1   relaxing   breathe   exciting   interesting   colourful

2   satellite   space station   hungry   space   rocket

3   fun   travel   study   float   live

3 💡 Draw paths and write. Then compare sentences with a partner.

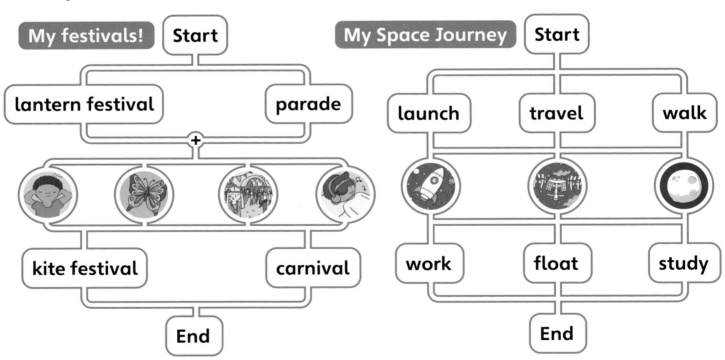

The lantern festival is more relaxing than the carnival.

The rocket travelled to the Moon. I floated.

_____   _____

Space Exploration

CULTURE 2: RUSSIA

1 Read about Russia again. Complete.

1 Size: Russia is _____ km². It's _____ !

2 Cities: the capital city is _____ .

3 Climate: It's very _____ in winter but hot in _____ .

4 Population: _____ people live in Russia.

2 Complete the sentences about World Space Week in Russia.

> look   Moon   watch

1 _____ astronauts returning from the ISS.

2 _____ at the stars.

3 Learn about the _____ .

3 Research World Space Week in your country. Answer, then talk to a partner.

1 When is World Space Week?

_____

2 What happens in your country?

_____

3 What events do you want to go to? Why?

_____

4 Read Min's diary entries. Which day was the best?

Day 1

It was the first day of Maslenitsa today. It was very exciting! The pancakes are the tastiest things ever!

Day 2

Today was even better than yesterday! We played a lot of games in the snow.

5 Think about a festival. Write diary entries for you.

5 Holiday time!

How can I design a beach?

1 Look and colour.

sand =

waves =

dolphin =

fish =

tree =

2 Which of these fish are not a pair? Circle.

CODE CRACKER

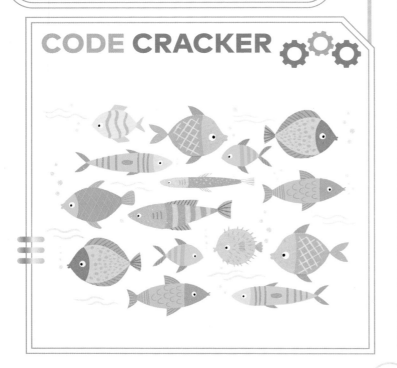

3 Listen to the song. Number the lines in order 1–8.

Verse 1

	We're going to a beach far away.
	Oh, happy days!
	Look at the sea and the waves.
	It's a warm, sunny day.

Verse 2

	Oh, happy days!
	We lie on the sand and play.
	We stay at a campsite.
	We watch the stars at night.

I can talk about holidays.

At the beach

VOCABULARY

I will learn beach words.

1 Complete. Then tick ☑ the activities you like.

> beach   boat trip   buy ice cream   campsite   dolphins   go surfing
> have a picnic   rocks   sand   sea   waves   whales

 **1** I play on the _____ and look at the _____ . ☐

 **2** We _____ on the beach. I _____ . ☐

 **3** He _____ in the _____ . ☐

 **4** I play in the _____ on the _____ . ☐

 **5** We go on a _____ and see _____ and _____ . ☐

 **6** We stay at a _____ on holiday. ☐

2 Choose things and activities from 1. Write, then compare with a partner.

EXTRA VOCABULARY

3 🎧 047 Look and write. Then listen and check.

 **1**    **2**    **3**    **4**

> seahorse   shark
> starfish   turtle

1 t_____   **2** s_____   **3** s_____   **4** s_____

I know beach words.

Language lab 1

GRAMMAR: I / YOU / HE / SHE / WE / THEY ...

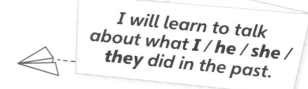

*I will learn to talk about what **I / he / she / they** did in the past.*

1 **Complete the sentences with the past of the action words.**

1 She _____ (buy) some sandwiches for our beach picnic.

2 I _____ (write) a postcard to my grandma on holiday.

3 We _____ (go) on a boat trip and _____ (swim) in the sea.

4 He _____ (read) his book on the beach.

5 They _____ (do) a lot of different things on holiday.

6 I _____ (see) a shark, so I _____ (run) out of the sea!

2 **Make a wheel of irregular action words.**

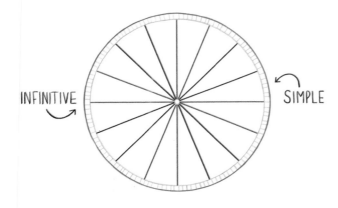

INFINITIVE   SIMPLE

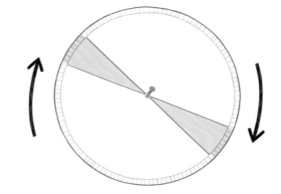

3 048 **Listen and match.**

1 Kerry   2 Abdul   3 Su

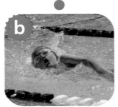
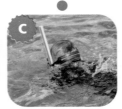

4 Rewrite the sentences in the negative form.

1 She went to the beach. _____

2 They had a picnic. _____

3 We saw dolphins. _____

4 I ate an ice cream. _____

5 You bought lunch in a café. _____

6 He swam in the swimming pool. _____

5 Find the path to the beach. You can only go on irregular action words.

CODE CRACKER

see	work	go	do	eat	study
read	have	buy	paint	write	live
play	walk	travel	want	swim	sit
float	start	launch	land	visit	get

6 Play *Word Tennis*. Take turns saying the past forms of the words from 5.

Story lab

> I will read a story and learn about helping.

1 🔧 049 Complete the speech bubbles. Then listen and match.

1 We put up our tents, _____ dinner and _____ to bed. There _____ a huge storm in the night. It was really scary!

2 Luckily, the next day was warm and sunny but we _____ and explore. There _____ plastic rubbish on the beach brought by the waves.

3 We helped to clean up the rubbish. We _____ a competition to see who collected the most! Then I heard a noise in a pile of rubbish.

4 I _____ a dolphin under the rubbish! Nadir got his mobile phone and called Whale and Dolphin Conservation.

5 They _____ really quickly! They _____ the dolphin back into the sea.

6 The Whale and Dolphin Conservation team _____ us ice cream and took us on a boat trip to say thank you. The dolphin said thank you, too!

a

b

c

d

e

f

2 💬 Act out the story in groups.

3 Read and answer.

1 Name three things the children saw on the beach:

_____ _____ _____

2 Name three things the children did at the campsite:

_____ _____ _____

3 Name two ways the Whale and Dolphin Conservation team said thank you: _____

_____

4 How do you think Freddie feels about the camping trip?
Circle: 😟 😐 😃 😄

5 What do you think was the best thing about the trip for Freddie?

_____

4 Complete Ellie's messages about the camping trip.

Day 1

We arrived at the campsite …

_____

_____

_____

Day 2

Guess what happened today!

_____

_____ _____

_____ _____

Values Ask for help.

5 Read and complete.

The last time I asked for help was _____ .

I asked _____ .

6 Make your own story book. ➡ page 119

I can read a story and learn about helping.

Phonics lab

*I will learn the **ar**, **ea** and **ee** sounds.*

1 🎧 050 Listen and tick ☑ . Then say.

1

arm   farm

2

sea   tree

3

beach   eat

2 🎧 051 Look and label. Then listen and say.

eat   feet   ice cream   park   sea   shark

1    2    3    4    5

_____   _____   _____   _____   _____

3 💡 🎨 Complete the poem. Use words that rhyme from 2.

In the _____ ,

I saw a _____ !

It wanted to _____

my _____ !

 the **ar**, **ea** and **ee** sounds.

Experiment lab

I will learn about the sea.

1 🎧 052 Listen and read about the sea again. Write.

> cold water   equator   North Pole
> South Pole   warm water

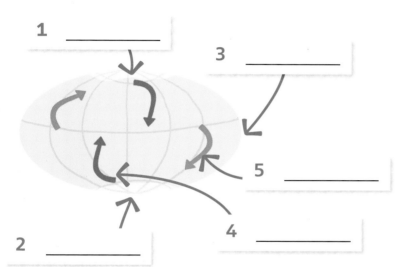

1 _____

3 _____

5 _____

4 _____

2 _____

2 Read and answer.

MATHS ZONE

The equator is 40,075 km long. 78.8 percent lies across the sea. What percentage lies over land? _____

The Arctic Circle is the invisible line around the North Pole. It is 16,000 km long. How much shorter is it than the equator? _____

EXPERIMENT TIME

Report

1 Complete and then compare with a partner.

1 Which colour water was warmer? _____

2 What happened to the warm water?

_____

3 What happened to the cold water? _____

4 Do you think the same thing happens to warm and cold air? _____

2 Write your report.

The warmer water floated to the top of the tank.

 about the sea.

Language lab 2

GRAMMAR: DID YOU / HE / SHE ...?

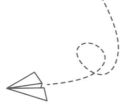

I will learn to ask about the past using **did**.

1 Read and write questions.

To: Erin Pearson | Subject: Beach trip

Hi Erin,

We're having a great holiday. We went to the beach yesterday. Grandma was very excited because it was her first ever time on a beach! She swam in the sea and played beach tennis with us. We had a picnic for lunch on the beach.

In the afternoon, we sat on the beach and relaxed. Then we went back to our tent. Grandma loved the beach, but she didn't like sleeping in a tent!

See you soon,

Finn

1 Where / go ? _____
We went to the beach.

2 Why / be excited ? _____
Because it was her first time on a beach.

3 What / have ? _____
We had a picnic.

4 Did / like ? _____
No, she didn't.

2 Listen and tick ☑.

	Have a good holiday	Have a picnic	Swim in the sea	Sleep in a tent	Go on a boat trip	See whales and dolphins
Ahmed						
Saskia						

3 Imagine you went on a beach holiday. Think of three things you did.

4 Ask and answer with a partner. Find out what they did.

I can ask about the past using did.

When did it happen?

COMMUNICATION

1 Read and number the texts in order.

After that, she gave us ideas about what we can do to help the plastic problem. ☐

Finally, we all asked questions. ☐

We watched a presentation about the seas. First, the teacher talked about sea creatures. ☐

Then she talked about plastic rubbish in the sea and on beaches. ☐

2 🎧 054 Listen and complete.

> clean the beach   give equipment
> go home   have a picnic   meet
> sort the rubbish

BEACH CLEAN-UP DAYS

We meet every Saturday!

10:00 a.m. _____

10:15 a.m. _____

10:30 a.m. _____

12:30 p.m. _____

1:30 p.m. _____

2:15 p.m. _____

3 💡 You did the activities in order. Write sentences in the past.

> swim in the sea   go on a boat trip
> play on the beach   buy ice cream
> have a picnic

First, _____.

_____

_____

_____

_____

Finally, _____.

4 💬 Give a list of activities to a partner to order.

I can talk about when things happened.

Design a shoebox beach

Project report

1 Think about your shoebox beach. Read and answer.

Did it ...

... have sand? _____

... have rocks? _____

... have surfers? _____

... have sea creatures? _____

... have a boat? _____

Other: _____

2 Complete your project report.

I went to a really cool beach. It was a *beautiful sandy beach with trees*. I went surfing and I saw a dolphin. I didn't sleep at the beach *because there wasn't a campsite*.

3 Present your project to your family and friends.

I stayed at the campsite. I went on a boat trip and saw a whale!

4 Think about your project and colour.

I can design a beach.

5 Write the past of the action words. Then write a sentence.

1 see _____
   ⊕ _____

2 eat _____
   ❓ _____

3 swim _____
   ⊖ _____

4 go _____
   ⊕ _____

5 write _____
   ❓ _____

6 have _____
   ⊕ _____

6 Read and answer about this unit.

BIG UNIT QUIZ!

1 Name four things you can see at the beach:
   _____ _____ _____ _____

2 Name four activities you can do on the beach:
   _____ _____ _____ _____

3 Write three words with ea: _____ _____ _____

4 Who found a fossil on a beach? _____

5 What did the warm water do in Experiment Lab? _____

7 Read and answer.

1 What's your favourite beach activity? _____

2 What's your favourite sea creature? _____

3 What was your favourite story frame? _____

Now go to your Progress Chart on page 4.

6 Let's shop!

How can I create a shop?

1 Look and label.

bookshop   greengrocer's   pet shop   supermarket

 1

 2

 3

 4

_____   _____   _____   _____

2 Look and sort.

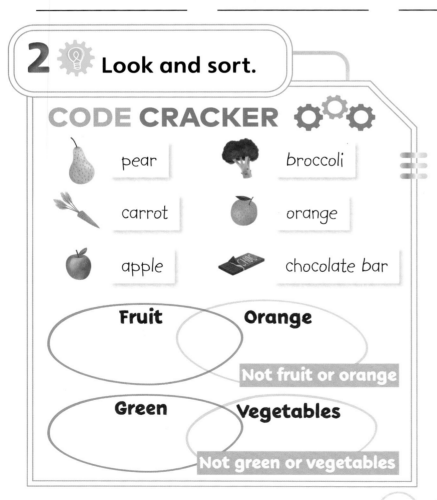

CODE CRACKER

pear

broccoli

carrot

orange

apple

chocolate bar

Fruit   Orange

Not fruit or orange

Green   Vegetables

Not green or vegetables

3 055 Listen to the song. Circle the shops.

Let's shop, shop, shop,

Until we drop, drop, drop!

Sweet shop, toy shop,

Amazing shops and more.

What a shopping centre –
let's go explore!

Let's shop, shop, shop,

Until we drop, drop, drop!

Bookshop, pet shop,

Amazing shops and more.

What a shopping centre –
let's go explore!

I can talk about shopping.

Where do we shop?

VOCABULARY

I will learn shopping words.

1 Where can you buy these things? Choose and write.

> bakery   bookshop   butchers   clothes shop
> department store   greengrocer's   market   pet shop
> shopping centre   supermarket   sweet shop   toy shop

1 burgers	2 notebooks	3 trousers	4 bananas	5 board game
_____	_____	_____	_____	_____
_____	_____	_____	_____	_____
_____	_____	_____	_____	_____
_____	_____	_____	_____	_____

2 🎧 056 Listen to the children and write.

Supermarket _____

_____ _____

Pet shop _____

_____ _____

Toy shop _____

_____ _____

3 Play *Three Things* in pairs.

EXTRA VOCABULARY

4 🎧 057 Look and match. Then listen and check.

1 cash register   _____

2 customer   _____

3 sales assistant   _____

4 stall   _____

I know shopping words.

Language lab 1

GRAMMAR: THERE IS A ...

I will learn to talk about amounts using **There is / are ...**

1 Sort the words.

> biscuit   cheese   egg   fruit   rice   salad
> salt   sandwich   sugar   sweets   tea   tomato

Countable nouns:	Uncountable nouns:
_____ _____	_____ _____
_____ _____	_____ _____
_____ _____	

2 Complete with some, any or a.

1 Have you got _____ bananas?

2 I've got _____ rice in the kitchen.

3 I didn't buy _____ pasta.

4 There aren't _____ books at the shop.

5 She wants _____ teddy bear.

6 They've got _____ bread.

3 🎧 058 Listen and tick ☑ or cross ☒.

① Claudia's List

apples ☐
water ☐
coffee ☐
chocolate ☐
grapes ☐

② Malek's List

salad ☐
tea ☐
pizzas ☐
sugar ☐
ice cream ☐

4 Make the connections. Use different colours. How many sentences can you make?

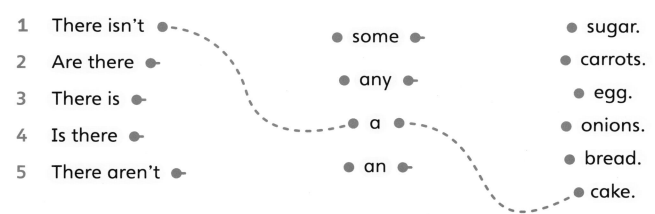

1 There isn't
2 Are there
3 There is
4 Is there
5 There aren't

some
any
a
an

sugar.
carrots.
egg.
onions.
bread.
cake.

5 Look around the classroom. Write sentences with some, any or a/an. Use these words or think of your own ideas.

> apple   books   boys   chocolate   desks
> elephant   pandas   rice   whiteboard

_____

_____

_____

_____

_____

6 Compare your sentences from 5 with a partner.

There's a whiteboard.

There are some books.

There aren't any elephants.

I can talk about amounts using There is / are …

Story lab

READING

I will read a story about a pet rabbit.

Runner Rabbit

1 059 **Number the story frames in order. Listen and check.**

2 Write a short summary of the story.

The children were at a pet shop and _____ .

_____ .

3 Complete the sentences. Who's speaking? Match.

1. Excuse me, have you got _____ rabbit food?

2. Yes, there's _____ over there.

3. Did you see _____ rabbit in the shop?

4. No, I didn't see _____ rabbits!

5. I'd like _____ carrots, please.

6. There are too _____ rabbits!

 a

 b

 c

 d

 e

4 ✹ Look at the ending of the story. Draw.

What's in the box, kids?

It's a present for you, Nadir!

It's an empty box …

Oh no, Runner Rabbit – not again!

Look! He's running to see Snowball!

5 ✹ Put a rabbit in a box. Act out.

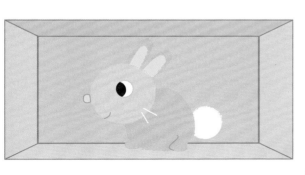

6 ✹ Write a new ending. ➔ page 125

It's a present for you, Nadir!

I can read a story about a pet rabbit.

*I will learn the **or** and **er** sounds.*

1 Complete the words with **er** and **or**. Then listen and say.

1 h____ ____se   2 c____ ____n____ ____   3 m____ ____ning

4 teach____ ____   5 sh____ ____t____ ____   6 fath____ ____

2 Choose and write six words. Play *Bingo*!

father	shorter	horse
mother	horn	corner
sister	bigger	morning

3 What comes next? Look and tick ☑ .

CODE CRACKER

a ☐

b ☐

I know the **or** and **er** sounds.

Experiment lab

DESIGN: BRAND DESIGN AND LOGOS

I will learn about brand design.

1 How do colours make you feel? Read and match.

red ●

blue ●

green ●

yellow ●

black ●

● 1 Friendly, young and sunny.

● 2 Classic, serious and mature.

● 3 Modern and expensive.

● 4 Loud, fun and modern.

● 5 Calm and natural.

2 Work in groups. Choose the best colour or colours for these products.

sugar-free fizzy drink

toothpaste

pasta

shampoo

kids' trainers

EXPERIMENT TIME

Report

1 Write about your experiment.

Describe the most popular design:

_____

Describe the least popular design:

_____

2 Write your report.

Most of the class liked our purple and yellow design the best.

 about brand design and logos.

Language lab 2

GRAMMAR: HOW MUCH / MANY ...?

*I will learn to talk about amounts with **a lot / lots of**, **much** and **many**.*

1 Read and number.

1 ➕ sentences with countable nouns use

2 ➕ sentences with uncountable nouns use

3 ➖ sentences with countable nouns use

4 ➖ sentences with uncountable nouns use

5 ❓ sentences with countable nouns use

6 ❓ sentences with uncountable nouns use

a many ____ ____   b much ____ ____   c a lot of / lots of ____ ____

2 Complete the sentences with a lot of, much or many.

1 We've got _____ oranges.

2 How _____ is this? It's ten pounds.

3 How _____ do you want? Six!

4 They eat _____ apples.

3 061 Listen and complete the quantities.

1

apples
____

eggs
____

coffee
____g

2

rice
____g

oranges
____

sugar
____g

4 Read and answer.

MATHS ZONE

One orange – 100g

One apple – 60g   One egg – 50g

How much does each list in **3** weigh?

_____

Which is the heavier list?

_____

I can talk about amounts with a lot , much and many .

Shopping

COMMUNICATION

I will learn what to say in shops.

1 Listen and number the shops.

2 Work in pairs. Choose a shop and write a dialogue.

Customer: _____

Salesperson: _____

Customer: _____

Salesperson: _____

Customer: _____

Salesperson: _____

Customer: _____

Salesperson: _____

3 Perform your conversation to the class. Guess the shops.

Excuse me, have you got any bread?

Bakery!

Yes, what type of bread would you like?

I know what to say in shops.

Create a shop in a shopping centre

Project report

1 Think about your project. Read and answer.

Did you create a department store, a shopping centre or a market? _____

List the different shops or stalls you had:

_____ _____ _____

_____ _____ _____

2 Complete your project report.

There are some clothes shops. There's a pet shop. There are two bookshops and there's a supermarket.

3 Present your project to your family and friends.

There was a bakery and a supermarket in our shopping centre.

4 Think about your project and colour.

I can create a shop.

5 Look and rewrite the sentences.

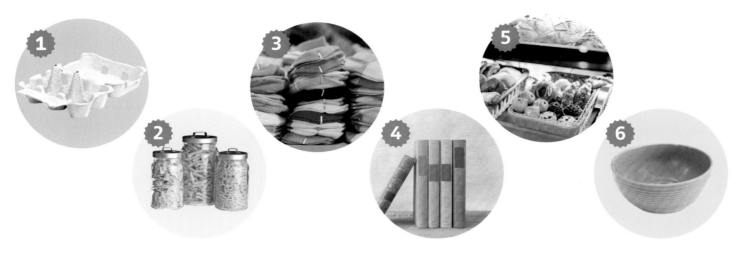

1 There are some eggs. _____

2 There isn't any pasta. _____

3 There aren't many socks. _____

4 There are a lot of books. _____

5 There isn't any bread. _____

6 There's a lot of rice. _____

6 Where are they? Listen and tick ☑.

7 Read and answer.

1 Where do you like to shop?

_____

2 What's your favourite shop?

_____

3 What's your favourite story frame?

_____

4 Which chocolate bar design do you like the most?

_____

Now go to your Progress Chart on page 4.

3 Checkpoint

UNITS 5 AND 6

1 Listen. Where were they? Tick ☑.

At a shopping centre ☐

At a beach ☐

2 Read and circle.

1 I bought much / some oranges.

2 We had / went a picnic on the beach.

3 How much / a lot of rice did you buy?

4 I didn't swam / swim in the ocean.

3 Draw paths. Then write.

My Holiday!

What did you see?

What did you do? Where did you go?

What did you do? Where did you go?

I saw a dolphin.

_____

I went shopping.

_____

I bought some chocolate.

_____

4 Compare sentences from 3 with a partner. Trace their path.

Beaches

1 Read about the UAE again. Answer.

1   What do the letters *UAE* stand for? _____

2   How many states are in the UAE? _____

3   What is the population of the UAE? _____

4   What is the weather like in the UAE? _____

2 Look, listen and write. Who bought the things? Was it Rashid (R), his mum (M) or his sister, Reem (S)?

 ☐    ☐    ☐    ☐    ☐

3 Read the dialogue. Which person from 2 is speaking to the salesperson?

A: Can I help you?

B: Yes, I'd like some apples, please.

A: Of course. How many would you like?

B: Six, please.

A: Anything else?

B: No, thank you. How much is that?

A: That's 20 dirham, please.

B: Thank you.

4 Think of a shop. Write your own dialogue with a salesperson.

5 Read your dialogue with a partner. Can they guess the shop?

7 Eco warriors!

How can I help the environment?

1 **Look and write. Then circle the things you recycle at home.**

1 **2**  **3**  **4** **5** **6**

1 p_____ _____ _____ _____ _____ _____   2 f_____ _____ _____

3 g_____ _____ _____ _____   4 t_____ _____ _____

5 p_____ _____ _____   6 m_____ _____ _____ _____

2 🎵 066 **Listen to the song. Match the pictures to the lines.**

We're going to be Eco Warriors!

1 We're going to save water in the shower. _____

2 We're going to clean up rubbish. _____

Eco Warrior power!

We're going to be Eco Warriors!

3 We're going to recycle plastic. _____

4 We're going to plant flowers and trees. _____

Eco Warriors are fantastic!

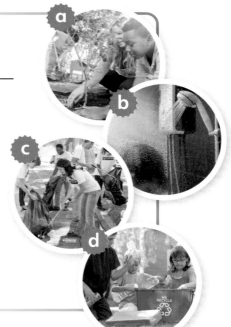

I can talk about the environment.

Caring for Earth

VOCABULARY

I will learn environment words.

1 Order the letters and write the words.

1 vironmenten _____   2 antpl _____

3 cycrele _____   4 durece _____

5 sueer _____   6 hsbrbui _____

7 stawe _____   8 lifwiled _____

2 Write words from 1 next to the definitions.

1 _____ : to use less of something so you don't create waste.

2 _____ : the things we throw away.

3 _____ : to use something again.

4 _____ : the world and nature around us.

5 _____ : to make rubbish into something new by changing its form.

3 Write definitions for the other words in 1 with a partner.

EXTRA VOCABULARY

4 Look and write. Then listen and check.

p_____   d_____   w_____   p_____

I know environment words.

Language lab 1

GRAMMAR: WHAT ARE YOU GOING TO DO?

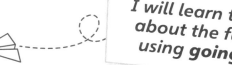

I will learn to talk about the future using going to.

1 Read and circle.

1   I / They am not going to waste water.

2   Are / Is Mike going to clean up rubbish?

3   She / We is going to save wildlife.

4   Am / Are they going to plant trees?

5   They / She aren't going to waste the green bottles.

2 🎧 068 Listen and tick ☑ for Shona (S), David (D), Tomas (T) and Aaliyah (A).

	S	D	T	A
Clean up rubbish				
Recycle				
Plant flowers				
Plant trees				
Save wildlife				

3 Look and match.

Aaliyah ●—

David ●—

Shona ●—

Tomas ●—

4 💬 Read and answer. Write two more questions. Then ask a partner.

1   What are you going to do tonight? _____

2   What are you going to do at the weekend? _____

3   What are you going to do to save the planet? _____

4   _____ ? _____

5   _____ ? _____

5 What is Ruby going to do on Saturday? Follow the sequence.

CODE CRACKER

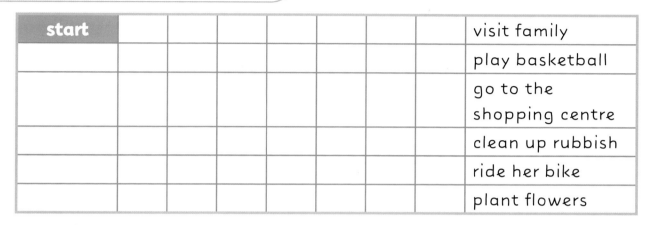

start								visit family
								play basketball
								go to the shopping centre
								clean up rubbish
								ride her bike
								plant flowers

2 → 2 ↓ 2 → 2 ↓ 1 ← 1 ↓ 3 → 1 ↑ 2 →

Ruby is going to _____ .

6 The sequence in 5 was too long. Write a shorter one.

_____

7 Read and answer.

MATHS ZONE

1 The village of Middleton recycled 10,000 tonnes of rubbish last year. The population of Middleton is 5000. Everyone recycles. How many tonnes does each person recycle on average? _____

2 The people of Middleton are going to recycle 25 percent more next year. How many tonnes are they going to recycle next year? _____

I can talk about the future using going to .

Story lab

READING

Eco Warrior Challenge

1 Who does the things in the story? Write, then listen and check.

 a

 b

 c

 d

1   Ellie _____

2   Max _____

3   Freddie _____

4   Yara _____

2 Who says these things? Write E (Ellie), F (Freddie), M (Max) or Y (Yara).

1 What am I going to do with all this rubbish? _____

2 I want to sort it out and recycle it. _____

3 No, we're not! The rabbits are going to eat all of the flowers! _____

4 I'm going to clean up the dirty empty land next door. _____

3 Read and circle T (True) or F (False).

1   The winner of the competition isn't going to win a prize.   T / F

2   The children are going to do different things.   T / F

3   Yara is going to use the old shopping trolley.   T / F

4   Nobody helps Freddie.   T / F

5   Max won the competition.   T / F

4 Look at Freddie's garden. Number in order.

5 What's Freddie's garden going to look like in the future? Draw.

One year

Ten years

6 Fill in the form for the Eco Warrior Challenge for you.

ECO WARRIOR CHALLENGE

NAME: _____   AGE: _____

What are you going to do?   _____

How are you going to do it?   _____

Who are you going to do it with?   _____

Do you think you are going to win?   _____

7 Make your own story book. ➡ page 121

 read a story about an eco challenge.

I will learn the short oo and long oo sounds.

1 🎧 070 **Circle the short oo words and underline the long oo words. Then listen and check.**

1
cook

2
food

3
Moon

4
good

5
wood

6
boot

2 🎧 071 **Listen, read and sing. Label the chants *long* or *short*.**

1 _____ oo

I go to school on the Moon.

The moon bus goes too fast.

We eat our food on the Moon.

We wear moon boots to play ball.

2 _____ oo

Take a look in a book.

Read a story or two.

It's good to learn about something new.

3 💡 **What comes next? Write words with the correct sound.**

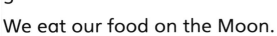
book   look   food   good   wood   zoo   cook

1 _____   2 _____

I know the short **oo** and long **oo** sounds.

Experiment lab

SCIENCE: DECOMPOSITION

I will learn about decomposition.

1 🔊 072 **Listen and read about rubbish again. Tick ☑ or cross ☒ .**

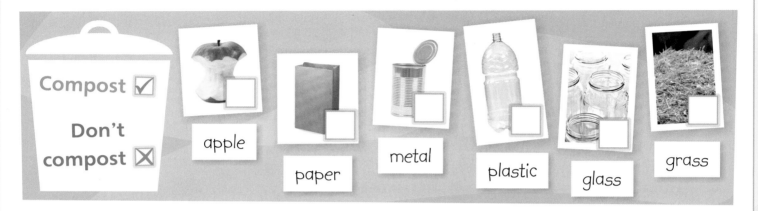

Compost ☑

Don't compost ☒

apple

paper

metal

plastic

glass

grass

2 Add more things to each group in 1.

EXPERIMENT TIME

Report

1 **Think and answer.**

What do you think each material is going to be like in …

one month?	one year?	ten years?
Apple: _____	Apple: _____	Apple: _____
Paper: _____	Paper: _____	Paper: _____
Plastic: _____	Plastic: _____	Plastic: _____

2 **Write your report.**

Apple
The apple was different. It was browner and softer.

_____
_____
_____

I know about decomposition.

Language lab 2

GRAMMAR: I WANT / WOULD LIKE TO ...

1 Read and write.

My Future Plans

When I'm older, I want to make a difference to the environment. I want to reduce the amount of plastic rubbish in the sea. I don't want sea creatures to die in dirty seas. I don't want to drive a car when I'm older because cars cause pollution. I'd like to be president so I can make rules to protect wildlife. I wouldn't like to live in a world without wildlife.

Lisa

She wants ...

She doesn't want ...

She wants ... 👍

She doesn't want ... 👎

2 🎧 073 Listen and complete.

1 _____ plant a lot of flowers.

2 _____ all the bees to die.

3 _____ any wildlife to die.

4 _____ save the rainforests.

3 How can you help the environment? Read and complete.

clean up rubbish   cycle to school   go in the car   help wildlife   recycle
reduce plastic   reuse things   save water   walk to school

1 I'd like to _____ every day.   2 I want to _____ more.

3 I'd like to _____ less.   4 I never want to _____ .

5 I wouldn't like to _____ .

I can talk about wants using I want / would like to ...

Future plans

COMMUNICATION

I will talk about weekend plans.

1 Complete the sentences with the correct form of going to. Listen and check.

A: What **1** _____ you _____ (do) at the weekend, Pam?

B: I **2** _____ (visit) my brother and his wife. They **3** _____ (move) house. I **4** _____ (not see) them for a long time after that.

A: Why's that?

B: Because they **5** _____ (not live) near here. What **6** _____ you _____ (do)?

A: I usually go to the cinema at the weekend but I **7** _____ (not go) this weekend.

B: Why not?

A: Because my dad **8** _____ (take) me to see a football match.

2 Read. Then look at the bar chart and label.

What are you going to do at the weekend?
Play computer games (PVG) ||||| |
Go to a restaurant (R) ||||
Visit family (VR) |||||
Do sport (PS) ||||| ||

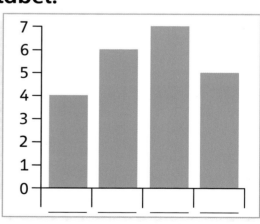

3 Think about four things you are going to do at the weekend. Then ask and answer to complete for a partner.

Are you going to go swimming?   Yes, I am.

I can talk about weekend plans.

Do a class environmental project

Project report

1 Think about your environmental project. Read and answer.

What are you going to continue doing:

every day? _____

every month? _____

at home or at school or on holiday? _____

Who is going to help? _____

What would you like to change after one month? _____

2 Complete your project report.

We planted flowers and put them in the classroom windows. We are going to water them every day.

3 Present your report to your family and friends.

This is our environmental project photo diary. We cleaned up rubbish from the park. We're going to do it every month.

4 Think about your project and colour.

I can help the environment.

5 Read and complete.

> dirty   environment   glass   paper   recycle   rubbish   wildlife

We went to the park yesterday and it was really **1** _____ with
2 _____ everywhere. We are going to go back tomorrow to clean it up
because it's dangerous to **3** _____ like birds and animals. There were a
lot of **4** _____ bottles and **5** _____ packaging everywhere. We
are going to **6** _____ all of it. It's good to help the **7** _____ !

6 Write sentences with going to.

> bake a cake   clean up rubbish   plant trees   watch a film

1 _____

2 _____

3 _____

4 _____

7 🌼 Draw around your hand. Write how you are going to save the planet. Make a class poster.

8 Read and answer.

1 What do you think is the best way to help the environment?

2 Which story character's eco project did you like the best?

Now go to your Progress Chart on page 4.

8 Let's work!

How can I create a careers fair?

1 Order the letters and write the jobs.

1 tecarchti _____

2 rechtea _____

3 rotcod _____

4 ramfer _____

2 Help the farmer plant corn. Look at the code below and complete the key. Colour.

CODE CRACKER

plant = ◯

start = ◯

end = ◯

skip = ◯

④ ◯ ② ◯ ③

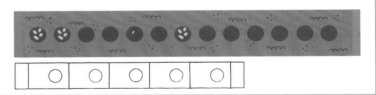

◯ ◯ ◯ ◯ ◯

3 Listen to the song. Number the lines in order 1–8.

075

Verse 1		Verse 2	
Do you want to be a doctor?	☐	I don't know yet!!	☐
Or a bank cashier?	☐	Do you want to be an architect?	☐
Do you want to be a nurse?	☐	Do you want to be a vet?	☐
Do you want to be a teacher?	☐	Do you want to be a farmer?	☐

I can talk about jobs.

Professions

VOCABULARY

I will learn job words.

1 Label, then number in alphabetical order.

_____

_____

_____

2 🎧 076 Listen and circle the jobs in 1.

EXTRA VOCABULARY

3 🎧 077 Listen, look and number.

A midwife

A plumber

A paramedic

An illustrator

I know words to describe jobs.

Language lab 1

GRAMMAR: I LIKE / DON'T LIKE ...

> I will learn to talk about my preferences using *I like / don't like ...*

1 Read. Correct the sentences.

1 She enjoying looking after animals.

   _____

2 They like to studying Maths.

   _____

3 We doesn't like working indoors.

   _____

4 He loves to reading books.

   _____

5 I don't liking coding.

   _____

6 Do you enjoy to speaking in class?

   _____

2 078 Listen and complete.

1 Sienna

enjoy	don't like
good at	not so good at

2 Bolin

enjoy	don't like
good at	not so good at

3 Write sentences about the children in 2.

Sienna

She enjoys looking after animals
and children.

_____

_____

Bolin

He enjoys listening to music and
doing sport.

_____

_____

4 Use the key to complete the text.

😃 = like 😍 = love 😞 = don't like 👍 = good at 👎 = not so good at

My mum works as a graphic designer. She 😍 **1** _____ (do) her job. She's 👍 **2** _____ (draw) and is very creative. She works from home. She 😃 **3** _____ (work) from home because she 😞 **4** _____ (travel) to an office. She 👎 **5** _____ (drive)! I 😍 **6** _____ (do) creative things like my mum. I want to be a graphic designer when I grow up!

5 💡 Look and sort for you.

CODE CRACKER ⚙️⚙️⚙️

code   cook   do maths   draw   look after animals
play a musical instrument   play computer games
ride a bike   study English   write

like doing

not so good at

Story lab

READING

I will read a story about growing up.

When I'm older ...

1 🔧 **Number the frames in order. Then listen and check.**

2 💬 **Retell the story in your words.**

3 Read and circle T (True) or F (False).

1 Yara doesn't like looking after kids.   T / F

2 Max is good at drawing.   T / F

3 Freddie and Nadir like the same things.   T / F

4 Nadir doesn't like studying Science.   T / F

4 Look and match.

5 Complete for Nadir. Then write for you.

I like _____ .
I love _____ and
I'm good at _____ .
I want to be a _____ !

I like _____ .
I love _____
_____ .
_____ !

6 Write a new ending. ➡ page 126

Phonics lab

OU / OW, OI / OY AND AY

> I will learn the **ou / ow**, **oi / oy** and **ay** sounds.

1 🔊 080 Listen and number. Then listen again and write.

a ☐

_____

b ☐

_____

c ☐

_____

2 Write the rhyming words from 1.

oi / oy _____ _____   ow / ou _____ _____

ay _____ _____ _____ _____

3 💡 Complete the poem with words that rhyme from 2.

I'm a happy _____ ,

This is my favourite _____ !

It's a little _____ ,

It lives in a little _____ .

It's _____ and grey.

I play with it every _____ .

I know the **ou / ow**, **oi / oy** and **ay** sounds.

Experiment lab

ENGINEERING: AUDIO ENGINEERS

I will learn about audio engineering.

1 081 **Listen about audio engineers again. Then look and number.**

a

b

____

____

c

d

____

____

EXPERIMENT TIME

Report

1 **Which guitar string makes the highest sound and which makes the lowest sound? Look and label *highest* and *lowest*.**

1 _____

2 _____

2 **Read and answer.**

MATHS ZONE

Sound travels in waves. A sound wave travels at 340 metres per second (m/s).

How far does sound travel in 6 seconds? _____

How far does sound travel in 1 minute? _____

2 **Write your report.**

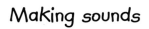

Making sounds

Thin elastic bands make a higher sound. Thick elastic bands make a lower sound.

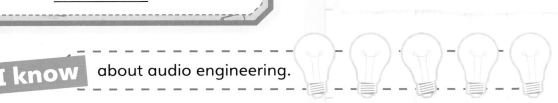

Language lab 2

GRAMMAR: WHY DO / ARE YOU ...

*I will learn to ask and answer questions using **Why** and **Because**.*

1 💡 **Read and match all possible answers.**

Why do you want
to be a computer
programmer? ●

- ● 1 Because I love coding.
- ● 2 Because I don't like sitting at a computer all day.
- ● 3 Because I'm good at using computers.
- ● 4 Because I like looking after animals.
- ● 5 Because I enjoy working outside.

2 **Write questions for the answers that didn't match in 1.**

_____

_____

_____

3 🎧 **Listen and complete. Then write F (Freya) or K (Kris).**
082

1 Why _____ ?
  - a Because I like looking after animals. _____
  - b Because I want to help the environment. _____

2 Why _____ ?
  - a Because I want to travel. _____
  - b Because I want to watch TV programmes in English. _____

3 Why _____ ?
  - a Because I like being fit and healthy. _____
  - b Because I like being part of a team. _____

4 Why _____ ?
  - a Because wildlife is dying out. _____
  - b Because of climate change. _____

I can ask / answer questions using Why and Because .

Giving opinions

COMMUNICATION

I will learn to give my opinion.

1 Write responses.   ☑ = agree   ☒ = disagree

1 I like doing graphic design.   ☑ _Me, too!_

2 I don't like studying Maths.   ☒ _____

3 I don't like watching TV.   ☑ _____

4 I love going to parties.   ☑ _____

5 I like swimming.   ☒ _____

6 I don't like shopping.   ☒ _____

I like doing graphic design.

Me, too!

2 🎧 Listen and read. Circle who likes both things.

Sally: I don't like doing maths problems.

Yusuf: Neither do I.

Kasia: Oh, I do!

Yusuf: I like looking after animals.

Kasia: Me, too.

Sally: I don't.

Sally

Kasia

Yusuf

3 Listen again and complete.

	Sally	Yusuf	Kasia
doing maths problems	🙁	◯	😀
looking after animals	◯	◯	◯

4 💬 ✂ Make a *Jobs Card* game. Agree and disagree with a partner.

I don't want to be a police officer.

I do!

I can give my opinion.

PROJECT AND REVIEW UNIT 8

Create a careers fair

Project report

1 Think about the jobs at your careers fair. Complete.

Architects like _____ .

Computer programmers are good at _____ .

Conservationists enjoy _____ .

Graphic designers are good at _____ .

Vets enjoy _____ .

Doctors like _____ .

Others: _____

2 Complete your project report.

Doctors like working with people. They are good at Science. They enjoy doing challenging things. Do you want to be a doctor?

Doctors enjoy doing challenging things.

Doctors are good at Science.

Doctors

Doctors like helping people.

Doctors like working with children.

Doctors love saving lives!

3 Present your report to your family and friends.

4 Think about your project and colour.

I can create a careers fair.

5 Read, choose and write.

I'm **1** _____ engineer. People always ask me **2** _____ I like my job. It's
3 _____ I **4** _____ designing things. I was very **5** _____ at Maths and
Science at school. I **6** _____ design technology lessons the best. I **7** _____
doing my job. The only thing I **8** _____ like is working very long hours!

1	a	the	b	a	c	an
2	a	what	b	why	c	because
3	a	like	b	because	c	too
4	a	love	b	don't	c	why
5	a	so	b	good	c	enjoy
6	a	hate	b	because	c	liked
7	a	love	b	don't	c	can
8	a	don't	b	hate	c	good

6 ◎ Choose which job you like best. Ask and answer with a partner. Use *Why* and *Because*.

> I want to be a computer programmer.

> Me, too. Why do you want to be a computer programmer?

> Because I like coding.

7 Read and answer.

1   What is your favourite job? _____

2   What are you good at? _____

3   What are you not so good at? _____

Now go to your Progress Chart on page 4.

1 🎧 084 Listen and write T (Teri), M (Mikael) or N (Nadia).

2 💡 Read and complete.

I'm very good **1** _____ coding, but I don't want **2** _____

be a computer programmer. I love being outside. This weekend I'm

3 _____ to plant some trees and flowers. I'd **4** _____

to be a scientist and study the environment.

3 💡 Write one sentence for each box. Then compare with a partner.

like

I

He

She

We

They

going to

want to

good at

She likes looking after animals and she's good at doing gymnastics.

Rainforests

1 Read about Peru again. Answer.

1   Which continent is Peru in? _____

2   Which famous forest is in Peru? _____

3   Which mountains are in Peru? _____

2 Read the email. Where did Lori visit?

To: grandma@grandma.com

Subject: Peru Holiday

Hi Grandma,

We're having a great time on holiday in Peru! Yesterday was the best day ever! We went to Machu Picchu, the lost city of the Incas.

We took a train from Cusco because Machu Picchu is high in the mountains. It is a very famous tourist site – millions of people visit Machu Picchu every year. The city is made of stone. It's almost 600 years old. It is the most beautiful place.

We are going to go to the Amazon rainforest tomorrow! I love travelling!

Lots of love,

Lori

3 Choose the picture of Machu Picchu to attach to the email.

4 Imagine you visit a famous place in your country. Write an email.

To:

Subject:

Use action words in the past to say where you went and what you did.

Use action words in the present to give facts and opinions.

Unit 1

**Look at the story on pages 16 and 17 of your Pupil's Book.
Then write your own story about a talent show.**

Written by:

_____

TALENT SHOW

Look at _____ .

_____ !

This is _____ . He

_____ .

A STORY ABOUT MY CLASS TALENT SHOW.

My class is practising.

Oh wow! Our teacher is _____ ! That's amazing!

This is _____ . She _____ .

This is _____ and _____ . They _____ .

It's the talent show today!

I _____ .

Unit 3

**Look at the story on pages 48 and 49 of your Pupil's Book.
Then write your own story about a class parade.**

Written by:

_____

My Class parade

We are having a parade.

It's very _____ .

Look at our _____ .
They are _____
and _____ .

A story about
my class parade

We are making _____ and _____ .

Oh wow! _____

That was the _____ ever!

One of the other groups is _____ .

Wow! Our class is the most _____ !

Unit 5

Look at the story on pages 80 and 81 of your Pupil's Book. Then write your own story about a beach holiday.

Written by:

_____

Our Class

Beach Holiday

Oh no! _____

We saw _____ .

_____

A story about a
beach holiday

We went to _____ .

Phew 😊! _____

_____

We went _____ . It was
_____ .

We _____ .

Unit 7

Look at the story on pages 112 and 113 of your Pupil's Book. Then write your own story about a challenge.

Written by:

_____

Our Eco Warrior Challenge

Oh, what a surprise 😶!
_____

_____

Another group wants to
_____.

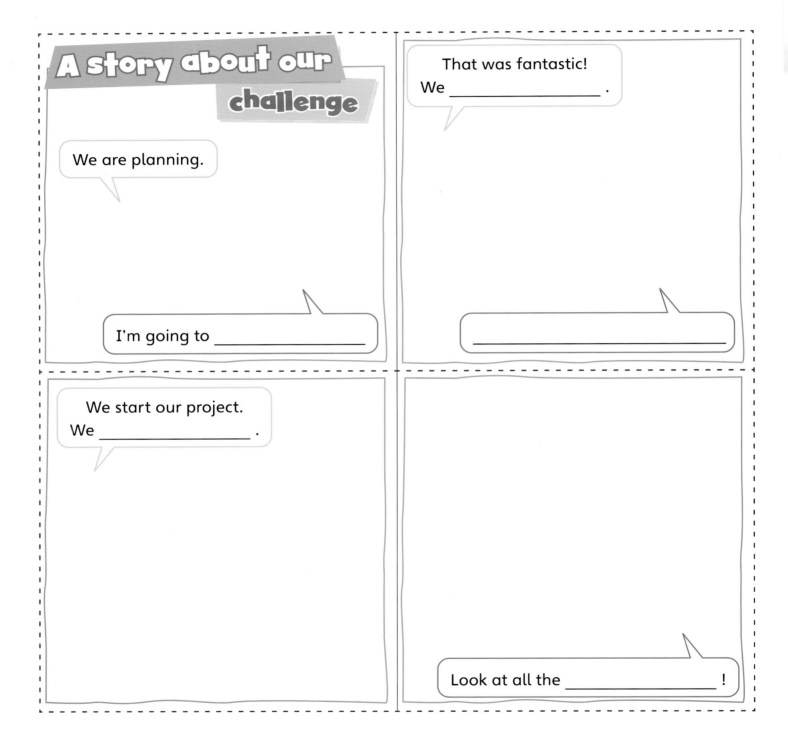

A story about our challenge

We are planning.

I'm going to _____

That was fantastic!
We _____ .

_____

We start our project.
We _____ .

Look at all the _____ !

Unit 2

The museum scare

Read the story and then make your own ending.

Unit 4

SPACE TRIP

Read the story and then make your own ending.

Unit 6

Runner Rabbit

Read the story and then make your own ending.

1

2 Quick! Follow that rabbit!

3 What can we call him?

I don't know, let's have a little look at him ... Oh no!

4 Did you see a rabbit in the shop?

No, I didn't see any rabbits!

Oh!

Excuse me, how much is that hat?

5

6

7

Unit 8

When I'm older ...

Read the story and then make your own ending.

Pearson Education Limited
KAO TWO
KAO Park
Hockham Way
Harlow, Essex
CM17 9SR
England

and Associated Companies throughout the world.

english.com/englishcode

First published 2021
Ninth impression 2023

ISBN: 978-1-292-32277-3

Set in Heinemann Roman 14 pt
Printed in Slovakia by Neografia

Acknowledgements

The publishers and author(s) would like to thank the following people and institutions for their feedback and comments during the development of the material:

Argentina

Maria Belen Gonzalez Milbrandt (Director Colegio Sol De Funes), Alejandra Garre (Coordinator Colegio San Patricio), Patricia Bettucci (Teacher Colegio Verbo Encarnado), Colegio Los Arroyos (Coordinator Luciana Pittondo), Instituto Stella Maris (Coordinator Ana Maria Ferrari), Gabriela Dichiara (Coordinator Nivel Pre-Primario En Escuela Normal N° 1 Dr Nicolas Avellaneda), Alejandra Ferreyra & Maria Elena Casals (Profesor Escuela Normal N° 1 Dr Nicolas Avellaneda), Maria Julia Occhi (Primary Director Colegio San Bartolomé Sede Fisherton), Gisele Manzur (English Director- Colegio Educativo Latinoamericano), Griselda Rodriguez (Ex-Directora de Instituto IATEL), Cultural Inglesa de Santa Fe (Olga Poloni y Silvia Cantero), Escuela Primaria de la Universidad Nacional del Litoral (Santa Fe) (Ricardo Noval, Natalia Mártirez y Romina Papini), Colegio La Salle Jobson Santa Fe (Santa Fe) (Miriam Ibañez), Colegio de la Inmaculada Concepción (Santa Fe) (Gabriela Guglielminetti), Colegios Niño Jesús y San Ezequiel Moreno (Santa Fe) (Ivana Serrano), Advice Prep School (Santa Fe) (Virginia Berutti), Centro de Enseñanza de Inglés Mariana G. Puygros (Santa Fe). Focus Group Participants: Alejandra Aguirre (Coordinator Colegio Español), Alicia Ercole (Director Instituto CILEL (Casilda)), Marianella Robledo (Coordinator Insituto CILEL (Casilda)), Viviana Valenti (Director Instituto Let's Go), Natalia Berg (Prof. Colegio de La Paz (San Nicolás)).

Turkey

Ugur Okullari, Isik Okullari, Doğa Koleji, Fenerbahce Koleji, Arı Okullari, Maya Okullari, Yükselen Koleji, Pinar Koleji, Yeşilköy Okullari, Final Okullari, Vizyon Koleji

Image Credits:

123RF.com: Aaron Amat 85, Alexandre Zveiger 25, Andrey Armyagov 49, Andriy Popov 101, Anna Om 96, Armen Bogush 18, 34, Artit Fongfung 85, Cathy Yeulet 88, 92, Darren Curzon 95, Evgeniya Nikitina 39, jirkaejc 85, Kaspars Grinvalds 101, 111, Konstantin Shaklein 49, 59, Marc Henauer 63, Meghan Pusey Diaz 23, Mykhailo Shcherbyna 89, Olena Zaskochenko 102, Robert Nieznanski 13, Rommel Canlas 107, serezniy 13, Singkam Chanteb 13, tan4ikk 24, thoermer 42, Tyler Olson 101, Wavebreak Media Ltd 101, yaavi 17; **Alamy Stock Photo:** Dorling Kindersley Ltd 20, NG Images 49, 59, SPUTNIK 50; **Getty Images:** AleksandarNakic/E+ 101, 105, 111, Alex Segre 35, anneleven/iStock/Getty Images Plus 63, Bettmann 50, chang 18, chris-mueller/iStock Editorial/Getty Images Plus 84, David Leahy/Cultura 110, ferrantraite/E+ 47, Fran Polito 17, Frans Lemmens/Corbis Unreleased 101, 105, 112, Fyletto/iStock/Getty Images Plus 63, georgeclerk/E+ 73, Hill Street Studios/DigitalVision 101, 111, ImagesBazaar 38, Interim Archives 50, JackF/iStock/Getty Images Plus 83, Jenny Dettrick/Moment 95, JESUSDEFUENSANTA/iStock/Getty Images Plus 35, John Foxx/Stockbyte 47, JohnnyGreig/E+ 109, Jose Luis Pelaez Inc/DigitalVision 98, Jose Luis Pelaez Inv/DigitalVision 49, Jose Luis Pelaez/Photodisc 110, jrroman/istock/Getty Images Plus 29, Jupiterimages/Stockbyte 34, kali9 105, KidStock/Photodisc 10, Klaus Vedfelt/DigitalVision 109, Laura Olivas/Moment 109, luckyraccoon/iStock/Getty Images Plus 83, Massimo Merlini/iStock Unreleased 47, Mikhail Japaridze 50, 50, Mint Images 25, Monty Rakusen 7, Monty Rakusen/Cultura 101, 105, 112, PeopleImages/E+ 63, 64, porkio photograph/Moment Open 47, Print Collector 35, Science & Society Picture Library 50, scyther5/iStock/Getty Images Plus 101, 101, SDI Productions/E+ 88, 112, sergeyryzhov/iSTock/Getty Images Plus 83, Stocktrek Images 49, 49, 59, 59, 59, Uraiwon Samatiwat/EyeEm 13, Westend61 63, 64, 101, 111, YinYang/E+ 101, 111; **Pearson Education Asia Ltd:** Coleman Yuen 107; **Pearson Education Ltd:** Jon Barlow 13, 18, 20, 21, 24, 25, 30, 31, 32, 33, 34, 36, 39, 46, 53, 57, 58, 72, 77, 79, 83, 84, 92, 96, 98, 109, Studio 8 18, Tudor Photography 69; **Pearson India Education Services Pvt. Ltd:** Nitin Tiwari 81 **Shutterstock.com:** 7, 34, 70, 101, 111, 448777 43, Aerostato 38, Africa Studio 13, 18, alejik 10, Alexander Raths 101, alice-photo 29, Andrey Armyagov 49, 59, antb 107, aphotostory 113, ArtmannWitte 64, AuntSpray 34, B Calkins 64, Butterfly Hunter 38, Castleski 48, Charles Brutlag 38, ChiccoDodiFC 29, Dan Tautan 23, Darren Baker 107, David Gilder 13, Didecs 43, Dim Dimich 17, Dr. Morley Read 89, Elena Schweitzer 43, Elena Sherengovskaya 92, Eric Isselee 38, Fer Gregory 48, foto76 95, Galyna Andrushko 23, Golubovy 105, Gorodenkoff 101, 111, HelloRF Zcool 25, Hung Chung Chih 42, J. Lekavicius 63, John A. Anderson 63, karamysh 25, Kolpakova Daria 58, lapandr 107, Larina Marina 71, Leszek Glasner 49, lilyling1982 37, Lipskiy 110, Lorraine Swanson 11, Luka70 23, LukaKikina 37, Lukas Gojda 123, 125, Mandy Godbehear 13, 18, 34, Marcio Jose Bastos Silva 29, Marcos del Mazo Valentin 63, Mega Pixel 95, Michael Smith ITWP 63, Mihai Blanaru 11, Montae 39, Morgan Lane Photography 88, Muellek Josef 42, Nagy-Bagoly Arpad 10, Natalin*ka 13, 18, 34, Nomad_Soul 83, Oleg_Yakovlev 48, oliveromg 64, oscar garces 37, Pajoy Sirikhanth 55, Pavel Vakhrushev 89, PEPPERSMINT 64, Picsfive 99, pixbox77 37, puthithons 88, Pyty 113, R. Gino Santa Maria 11, ra3rn 42, racorn 7, Rawpixel.com 42, 42, 92, Richard Peterson 38, Robbi 20, 32, 46, 55, 58, 72, 84, 98, 110, robuart 39, Romija 35, Runrun2 95, Ruth Black 38, Sedova Elena 17, Sergey Nivens 11, Sergey Novikov 42, 99, Shebeko 85, Siriporn-88 85, SkillUp 17, 20-21, 29, 32-33, 35, 43, 46-47, 55, 58-59, 61, 69, 72-73, 84-85, 87, 95, 98-99, 107, 110-111, 113, Sorbis 83, Stock Up 110, stockyimages 37, Sviatlana Sheina 10, Syda Productions 42, TerraceStudio 43, Thomas Bethge 85, Timofeev Sergey 95, Traveller Martin 49, Tyler Olson 101, vadim kozlovsky 89, VaLiza 13, Vasyl Shulga 107, vchal 34, Vitalii Smulskyi 18, Vladi333 48, VOJTa Herout 113, wavebreakmedia 101, welcomia 101, yanami 43, Yurly Golub 101, Zhu Difeng 102

All other images © Pearson Education

Animation screen shots
Artwork by Lesley Danson/Bright Agency, production by Dardanele Studio

Illustrated by:
Julia Castaño/Bright Agency, p.6; Sophie Crichton, pp.7, 30, 34, 60, 62 (top), 69, 76, 81, 86-87, 112; Lesley Danson/Bright Agency, pp.9, 14, 21, 26-27, 33, 34, 40-41, 52-53, 66-67, 73, 78-79, 93, 104-105, 123-126; Cathy Hughes/Beehive illustration, pp. 32, 41, 57, 59, 72, 79 (bottom); Sam Loman/ Bright Agency, pp. 23 (1.2-3), 28 (bottom), 33, 56 (bottom), 68 (middle), 82, 86; Lucy Semple/Bright Agency, pp. 22-23, 27 (2a,b), 33, 34, 43, 48 (middle), 49, 59, 64, 68 (bottom), 74, 82, 85, 88, 90-91, 106; Emma Trithart/Bright Agency, pp.8, 19, 46, 54 (centre, bottom), 56 (top), 75; Amy Wilcox/Lemonade Illustration Agency, pp.10, 12, 17, 44, 48 (top), 62 (bottom), 88, 100.

Cover Image: Front: **Pearson Education Ltd:** Jon Barlow